THE KING AND THE KINGDOM

THE KING
AND THE KINGDOM

WILLIAM BARCLAY

BAKER BOOK HOUSE
Grand Rapids, Michigan

PHOTOLITHOPRINTED BY CUSHING - MALLOY, INC.
ANN ARBOR, MICHIGAN, UNITED STATES OF AMERICA

ACKNOWLEDGMENTS

THIS book was originally published as a Bible Class Handbook for the Boys' Brigade, and the author and publisher wish to record their indebtedness to the Boys' Brigade for their co-operation in permitting this revised and amended edition to be published for use by young people and their elders throughout the Church at large.

The author and publisher acknowledge with appreciation permission to quote from the following copyright sources:

Messrs Methuen & Co. Ltd. for the poems, "Halfway up the Stairs" from *Now We are Six* by A. A. Milne, and "The Ways" from *Bees in Amber* by John Oxenham.

Messrs Harper & Row for lines from the poem "Gambler" from *Quotable Poems* by G. A. Studdert-Kennedy.

The scripture quotations in this publication, with a few exceptions, are from the Revised Standard Version of the Bible, copyrighted 1946 and 1952.

CONTENTS

PART IV

CHRIST THE KING

GENERAL INTRODUCTION

THIS book is a closely integrated whole. It begins with the time when the people of Israel had no king and when their king was God. The technical name for that is that Israel was a *theocracy*. Other nations might be *aristocracies*, where government was by the best people, or *oligarchies*, where government was by the chosen few, or *democracies*, where government was by the people; but Israel began by being a theocracy, a nation in which God was the direct and only king. The next stage was that the exigencies of life demanded some single human person who would be the focus of the life of the nation and the commanding voice in any emergency. Leadership became essential. So then we look at Saul, the first of the kings, who began so fairly and who ended in tragedy. Then we look at David, under whose rule the people of Israel really became a nation. Then we look at Solomon, that extraordinary mixture of wisdom and folly, who at one and the same time, made Israel a great nation and sowed the seeds of degeneracy and decay. After Solomon the nation split into two under Rehoboam. One half became the Northern Kingdom under Jeroboam, the other, the Southern Kingdom under Rehoboam. From the history of the Northern Kingdom we take the figure of the great prophet Elijah and then we move on to see the destruction of Samaria and the final obliteration of that part of the Kingdom. From the Southern Kingdom we take the figure of Hezekiah and then we move on to the fall of Jerusalem and the Exile. The Southern Kingdom did not disintegrate as the Northern Kingdom did. Away in far-off Babylon these Jews remained stubbornly and unalterably Jews. So we look at the exile and then we look at the return to Jerusalem under Ezra and Nehemiah. By that time Israel was a very little nation and she was directly between the two great world powers of Egypt and Assyria, and she experienced to the full the perils and the tribulations of her position. We see her in the terrible days of Antiochus Epiphanes, who made a deliberate attempt to wipe out the

Jewish faith and to destroy the very name of Jehovah. And then we take a quick view of the follies and the mistakes and the tragedies which ended in the destruction of Jerusalem in A.D. 70 and wrote "finis" to the Jews as a nation. It is to be noted that that period between the Old and the New Testaments is seldom taught; and yet without a proper understanding of it the actual history of New Testament times is not fully intelligible.

We then turn from the events of history to the thoughts and the conceptions behind history. We look at the Jewish ideas of the Kingdom and of the golden time to come. It was against all this background that Jesus lived and taught. It was into this world of history and thought that he came. We look at Jesus' idea of the Kingdom. We see that to him basically the Kingdom was a society upon earth where God's will is as perfectly done as it is in heaven. We see the passports to the Kingdom as Jesus saw it—the childlike spirit, the forgiving spirit, the serving spirit. We see the supreme worth of the Kingdom, the necessity of decision and the necessity of effort. We see the things that hinder a man's entry into the Kingdom.

Having then studied the Kingdom, we turn to the King himself, and we try to understand the Birth of the King, the Death of the King, the Resurrection of the King, and the final Triumph of the King. That is the general scheme of this book and it is plain to see that it is a closely wrought whole with a line of thought and of events running all through it.

WILLIAM BARCLAY

PART I

NO KING BUT GOD

The Centre of Everything

When we are listening to sermons in Church or when we are sharing in prayers when we worship, there is no phrase that we hear oftener than the phrase, The Kingdom of God. All through this book we are going to think of God's Kingdom and of God's King. We are going to see how bit by bit the idea of having a king came to God's people Israel; how earthly kings rose and fell, some of them good and some of them bad; how the people dreamed of the Kingdom which some day God would give them; how Jesus, God's Anointed King, came into the world, and how he told us about the Kingdom that was his.

In the Days when there was no King

We must begin a long way back in history. The father of the people Israel, the founder of the nation was Abraham and Abraham lived away back about 2500 B.C. Bit by bit throughout the years and the centuries Abraham's descendants increased and increased until they became the people Israel. But it was a long time before they had a king. Their first king was Saul, whose life we shall soon be studying, and Saul's date is about 1040 B.C. That is to say, for almost 1,500 years the nation of Israel had no king at all. That is one way of putting it; but although they had no earthly king they nevertheless had a King who was not of this earth. One of their great heroes was Gideon. Gideon lived round about 1200 B.C. You can read his story in Judges, chapters 6, 7 and 8. In his day the great threat and trouble to the Israelites was the Midianites. They lived on the other side of Jordan in the eastern country; and the eastern country was a desert. They were really Arabs and they used to cast longing eyes at the country west of the Jordan where the Israelites lived for it was a fertile land.

Worse than that, every springtime they used to descend on
Israel and steal their crops and plunder their towns and
villages and make life a misery. It was then that Gideon,
called by God, arose and with a great victory drove back
the Arabs and delivered his country. Now, as you would
expect, his countrymen were very grateful to him and they
came to him with an offer (Judges 8:22, 23). They said to
him, "You have delivered us from the hands of these Arabs
who were ruining our country and our lives. Come and be
our king and you, and after you, your sons, will rule us." And
Gideon said, "No; neither I nor my sons will ever rule over
you. *The Lord shall rule over you.*" For Gideon the only
king was God. For over 1,500 years the only king the Israelites
had was God. That does not mean that every man, woman
and child in Israel was true and faithful and loyal to God;
but it does mean that there were always great and noble and
heroic men, who kept the nation in the way that God meant
them to take, and who made them, often against their will,
take God's way.

God the only King

When a king or queen of this country is crowned there
comes a part in the coronation service when the monarch's own
brothers and when all the great ones of the land take a promise
in words like this: "I do become your liege man of life and
limb, and of earthly worship, and faith and truth will I bear
unto you, to live and die against all manner of folks, so help me
God." It is a promise of perfect loyalty and perfect service to the
king or to the queen. That is the way that the Israelites felt
towards God. He was their king. They would give their loyalty
and their allegiance to no one else. Now let us see what it meant
that God was their only king.

Going where God sent them

Because the Israelites looked on God as their king it meant
that *they were ready to go wherever God sent them*. That is what
Abraham began by doing. Abraham had a very comfortable
life in Haran, but the command of God came to him, "Go from

your country and your kindred and your father's house to the land that I will show you" (Gen. 12:1). Abraham lived among a heathen people and if he was really going to serve God he had to leave it all behind. It was hard but God said to him, Go, and in obedience Abraham went out not knowing where he was to go (Hebr. 11:8). It was the same with Moses. Moses was brought up as a royal prince of the house of Egypt. But God said to him, I want you to leave all this and to lead my people out of Egypt, through the desert, into the promised land. It was hard, but God said to Moses, Go, and in obedience he went.

All the really great men have been like that. One of the greatest saints of modern times was Dr. Albert Schweitzer. Even when he was a boy he said, "As far back as I can remember the thought of all the misery in the world has been a constant source of pain and grief to me." He was a brilliant boy and a brilliant student. He became a Doctor of Philosophy. He was a professor in Strasbourg University. He was a magnificent organist, the greatest authority on the music of Bach in the world. And then he began to hear of the miseries of the natives in Central Africa. He said to himself, "I must do something about this." Dropping all his other work, he took his degree as a doctor and his wife trained as a nurse, and the two of them gave up everything and went away to Lambarene in Africa to open a hospital to help the poor Africans who lived there. It was hard. It was hard to give up a life of fame and comfort and ease to go away to the hardships and the difficulties and the dangers of Africa, but God said to Albert Schweitzer, Go, and in obedience he went.

We have all got to choose what we are going to do with our life. We can do it in two ways. We can say, Where can I get the best pay, the easiest job, the most comfortable life? Or, we can say, Where can I be of most use? What does God want me to do? If God is really our king, we will say to him, Where do you want me to go?

Doing what God commands

Because the Israelites looked on God as their king *they were ready to do whatever God commanded them to do*. Through

Moses they received the commandments of God and they were ready at least to try to keep them. There are really only two kinds of people—those who make it the business of their lives to do what they want to do; and those who make it the business of their lives to do what God wants them to do.

Let us go back to a summer day in the year 1882. The Australian cricket team are playing at Cambridge against Cambridge University. Many people are angry that the match is on at all because the Australians have not lost a match and they think that Cambridge will be so heavily defeated that they will be completely disgraced. Just walking in from the wicket there is a young Cambridge student, six feet tall; and the ground is ringing with cheers for C. T. Studd is walking in after scoring 101 runs. The Australian team has batted and collapsed and once again the ground is ringing with cheers for C. T. Studd has taken eight wickets. The next morning comes and Cambridge are batting. There is the click of the bat and the flash of the scarlet ball and C. T. Studd has made the winning hit and Australia has been beaten for the first time on their tour by Cambridge University. That is the kind of man C. T. Studd was. He was the greatest cricketer of his day. His father was wealthy and C. T. Studd met Jesus Christ and became a Christian. He knew life could not be the same. He was reading his Bible one day. He came to the text, "Ask of me and I will give thee the heathen for thine inheritance and the uttermost parts of the earth for thy possession" (Ps. 2:8). And C. T. Studd knew that he must become a missionary for Christ. Everyone tried to stop him. His closest friends were all against it; but that is what God was telling C. T. Studd to do and he did it. Later C. T. Studd's father died. He left him more than £25,000. But the Bible said, "Go thy way, sell whatsoever thou hast and give to the poor" (Mark 10:21). C. T. Studd sat down and made out some cheques—£5,000 to D. L. Moody, £5,000 to General Booth, £5,000 to George Muller, £5,000 to the Whitechapel Mission and another five cheques each for £1,000. When the estate was finally settled he discovered—to his horror—that he still possessed £3,400. He offered the money to his wife. She would not take it. He wrote to General Booth,"I am instructing our bankers to sell out our last earthly investments and to give them to you; henceforth our bank is in heaven. Now we can thank God that we are in the proud position of being able to say, 'Silver and gold have I none.' " He made only one condition; that Booth should never say who had given the money. As C. T. Studd saw it, that is what God had commanded him to do— and he did it.

Sometimes we should examine ourselves. We say that Jesus is our Master and our King. We say that he is our pattern and our Lord. But when it comes to actual facts and actual choices on what principle do we act? Do we say to ourselves, Well, what do I want to do? Or, do we say to God, Lord what do you want me to do? If God is really our king we will always be ready to do what God commands us to do.

Being what God desires

Because God was their king *the Israelites were ready to be what God desired them to be.* Now this was really difficult, because it meant that they had to be different from all other peoples. Often they are called a *holy* people. This word *holy* really means different. When the Bible speaks of God as *holy* it really means that God is quite different from men; that he lives a different kind of life and has a different kind of being; and when God commanded the Israelites to be a *holy* people it meant that they had to be different from all other nations. Other nations might worship more than one God; they could only worship Jehovah. Other nations might have their graven images and their idols to make worship easier; they could not have these things. Other nations might have a much laxer and lower standard of morality; they must keep themselves clean and pure. Inevitably they would be thought a queer, strange nation; inevitably they would be unpopular and disliked. But it was God's command and they were ready to face it all.

The one thing that most of us fear to be is to be different from others. It is much easier to do what other people do and to go with the crowd and to conform to the things the world does. But if we are really honest when we say that

God is our king it means that we must not hesitate to be different from others if need be. Jesus told his disciples, "Do not think that I have come to bring peace on earth; I have not come to bring peace, but a sword" (Matt. 10:34). In the early days of the Church that was true, for often when a man became a Christian his family put him out and would have nothing to do with him and it was as if a sword had cut him off from his nearest and dearest. It is still like that in the mission field. Often being a Christian is like having the closest ties in life cut by a sword. It will not likely be so bad as that for us; but the fact remains that often if we are to be true to God we have to be different from others. There are things they can do that we cannot do; there are ways in which they can behave that we cannot accept; there are pleasures they can take that are forbidden to us; there are ways of speaking that they will allow but which we must never use. It is difficult; but nothing is too hard to do in order to be true to the King of kings.

No King but God

For long centuries the Israelites had no king but God. That meant that they were ready to go where God sent them; to do what God commanded them; to be what God desired them to be. And if God is really to be our King we must give him a loyalty, a love and an allegiance like that.

QUESTIONS FOR DISCUSSION

1. How can I know what God wants me to do?

2. In what ways must a Christian be different?

3. Will obedience to God necessarily mean for me that I have to leave my present place in life?

PART II

THE HUMAN KINGDOM

1. SAUL, THE KINGLY FAILURE

(The material for the life of Saul is in 1 Samuel 8, to the end of the book. When 1 Samuel was written, many stories were current about Saul and about David, and they were often told from different points of view. The writer of 1 Samuel has told us all the stories which came down to him. We have simply taken them as they stand and have tried to weave a connected narrative out of them.)

The Need for a King

We have seen how for many years and centuries the Israelites had no king but God. Throughout these years they believed that only God had a right to that supreme title. But difficulties confronted them. Even after they had settled down in the Promised Land life was dangerous. They were surrounded on all sides by enemies. From east of Jordan there were the Arab tribes, the Midianites and the Amalekites; from the west there came the Philistines. Life was one long battle and one long warfare. To cope with such a situation it was necessary that the nation should have one commander who would take charge of things and whose word would be law. So in the very nature of things, compelled by the circumstances in which they found themselves, they were forced to choose a king. There were those who felt that by so doing they were doing wrong and were despoiling God of his rightful title and his rightful honour, but in the circumstances they could not do other than choose a king.

The Man with every Advantage

The choice fell upon Saul. He was of the tribe of Benjamin and his father was called Kish; and he started out with every advantage. He was "a handsome young man. There was not a man among the people of Israel more handsome than he;

from his shoulders upward he was taller than any of the people"
(1 Sam. 9:1, 2). The end was to be tragedy but Saul started out
with every chance.

Saul finds a Kingdom

1 Samuel 9 tells how Saul found his kingdom. His father's
herd of asses had wandered away and got lost and Saul and his
servant set out to find them. Far and wide they sought for them
and could not find them; and then they remembered Samuel the
wise man and thought that he could help them. They went to
him for advice; and in this tall and splendid young man Samuel
saw the man whom God had chosen, and, before they parted
from him, Saul had been anointed king. Saul was the man who
set out to look for a herd of asses and who found a kingdom.

Saul found his kingdom all in the day's work. It is in the
faithful performance of the ordinary routine, often unin-
teresting, everyday things, that the greatest things are done.
One day there appeared in a Chicago daily paper an advertisement offering a reward of five thousand dollars for any
information which would lead to the arrest of the murderer of
Police Officer Lundy. A reporter saw the advertisement and
was interested. He looked up the case and found that, twelve
years before, a lad called Majec had been arrested and imprisoned for the murder of Lundy, but that the evidence had
been very doubtful and the justice of the verdict very open to
question. He went to the address from which the reward had
been offered. He found it in a very poor district behind the
Chicago stockyards. The door was opened by an old woman,
neat and clean, but obviously very poor. The reporter talked
to her. She proved to be Majec's mother; she had never believed that her son was guilty; she was determined to prove
him innocent and had offered this reward. "But," said the
reporter, "five thousand dollars is a lot of money. How did
you get it? How can you offer all that?" She answered in
one sentence, "I scrubbed floors." For twelve years, eight
hours a day, five days a week she had scrubbed and had saved
and saved until she had the money for the reward. The upshot
was that the newspaper took up the case and her son's

innocence was proved and he was released. She had done this tremendous thing by scrubbing floors, by doing the routine thing and doing it faithfully and well. She succeeded in this great achievement simply by doing the day's work.

Saul found a kingdom all in the day's work. If we want to make something big out of life we shall do it, not by dreaming about great things, but by doing the little things faithfully and well.

The Impatience of Saul

So Saul was eager to set out on his campaigns to liberate his country from the fear of her enemies. But Samuel had given him an order. He told him to wait at Gilgal until he should come and until the necessary sacrifices had been truly and properly made (1 Sam. 10:8). But Saul was impatient and he went out to battle before Samuel came (1 Sam. 13:1-14). Samuel was very blunt with him. He told him that he had spoiled everything; that his kingdom would not continue.

The downfall had begun and the tragedy was under way. Saul had shown himself impatient and headstrong and unfit to be a king. He who had begun with all advantages was on the way to ruin. It is easy to condemn Saul, but we are all very likely to do the same. We would very quickly condemn a ship's master who sailed without waiting for the weather report; or the pilot of a plane who took off without waiting for information about the weather conditions. If a storm blew up and the ship or plane was wrecked, we would say that the man had no right to be so impatient; he should have waited. Very often we are so impatient that we reject the advice of those who are older and wiser than we are. Very often we are so impatient that we reject the guidance of Jesus or that we never ask for it. That kind of impatience was the first step in the downfall of Saul; and it can bring us into all kinds of trouble, too.

The Disobedience of Saul

But Saul did not learn from his foolishness. He went out on a campaign against the Amalekites. Now Samuel gave him orders that everything belonging to the Amalekites should be destroyed. It sounds hard; after Jesus came, men knew that there was a better way than the way of slaughter and of force; but in those days men were terrified that there might come into the life of Israel even the faintest taint or infection of anything evil; so they safeguarded themselves and the purity of the nation by refusing to touch anything which had belonged to heathen lands. But Saul broke the commandment. Instead of destroying everything he kept the best of the spoil (1 Sam. 15:1-23). Saul was rebuked by Samuel and Samuel told him that for his disobedience God had rejected him from being king.

Of all qualities for the success of life that which is most essential is obedience. The long training that a soldier has to do and all the drill that he has to go through, is all designed with one end in view—that when the command comes he should automatically obey. Every day and every hour of the day God tells us what he desires us to do, for the voice of conscience always speaks in our hearts. And there can never be any happiness in life when we are doing things against God. The first question that the Christian must always ask is, Lord, what do you want me to do?

The Jealousy of Saul

By this time things were going from bad to worse with Saul. There had come to him a trouble of the mind. The only thing which would soothe this trouble was music. So they sought one who was skilful in playing on the harp so that when the black mood came upon Saul he might be soothed by the music. They found such a one in David, the son of Jesse, and so he came to Saul so that he might bring him relief in his trouble (1 Sam. 16:14-18). But bit by bit David grew to greatness. He became the great leader and the great warrior and he became the hero of the people for his gallant exploits. So one day after one of his audacious forays, David came back and Saul was there; and women had come out to meet them and to greet them with songs; and the song they sang was, Saul has slain his thousands but David his ten thousands (1 Sam. 18:5-9). And immediately there was born in Saul's heart a demon of jealousy. Twice Saul tried to kill David. He hurled a spear at him as David played and sought to pin him to the wall, but David escaped (1 Sam. 18-10, 11). Again he tried to murder David (1 Sam. 19:8-11) and David had to flee for his life. But Saul was now a brooding, dark, unhappy man with this spirit of jealousy gnawing at his heart.

Jealousy is an ugly sin. Jealousy means that we grudge the other person his or her happiness and prosperity and success. We must always remember one thing—our job in life is not to envy others their possessions, their gifts or their qualities, but to do the best we can with ourselves as we are. One thing will make that easier—always to remember that God has something for us to do which no one else can do, a task which is specially our task, a duty which is uniquely our duty. Where God has set us, with the gifts and the talents and the possessions God has given us, there we must do with our might what our hands find to do, and never think of the things that others have which we do not possess, or the things which cannot be for us.

The final Tragedy

By this time Saul was an unhappy man. He knew that he had failed. And so there came the last battle. The Philistines had arrayed themselves against Israel and had come north to Mount Gilboa. Saul began the battle in the wrong spirit because he began afraid (1 Sam. 28:5). So the battle closed up among the mountains and Saul's three sons were killed and he was wounded. With the battle lost and life ebbing away and nothing left to live for, Saul bade his armour-bearer to kill him; but the armour-bearer could not do it; so Saul took his own life and fell upon his sword and committed suicide (1 Sam. 31:1-6). The life that had begun so fairly ended in tragedy.

The kingly Failure

Saul had begun life with every chance. Everything seemed set fair and he seemed to have every qualification for success and honour. In body Saul was head and shoulders taller than all his fellow men; but there was something amiss in his heart and his mind and his soul: Saul was impatient; Saul was disobedient; Saul was jealous; and because of these faults the life which might have been so glorious ended in shame. And in that the life of Saul is a warning to each one of us.

QUESTIONS FOR DISCUSSION

1. What makes it difficult for me to ask and to accept advice?
2. How do I find out what Jesus wants me to do?
3. How can I stop myself being jealous?

2. DAVID, FROM SHEPHERD LAD TO KING

(The material on David has been divided into two chapters. The first simply tells the story of David: the second attempts to describe those characteristics which made David great. The reason for adopting this course is twofold. First, the story of David is in itself one of the world's great stories and should be studied as an unbroken and connected narrative. Second, there is little point in talking about the characteristics of David without a foundation of the knowledge of the life of David; and that life loses half its interest and its thrill if the telling of it is broken up to insert the lessons of it in the midst of the narrative.)

The Shepherd Lad is chosen

There came a time in the life of Saul when it became tragically clear that Saul was a man who had taken on a job that was too big for him. More and more clearly he was a failure as a king. So Samuel, the great prophet, who was the guide of the nation, was moved by God to search for someone who might some day soon take the mantle of kingship upon him. God sent him to the household and the family of Jesse. One by one seven of Jesse's sons passed before him, all splendid young men, but Samuel knew that the choice of God had fallen on none of them. He asked Jesse if he had no more sons and Jesse replied that only the youngest was left and he was a shepherd lad out on the hillside with the sheep. Samuel insisted that this lad should be sent for. His name was David; and when David came in, ruddy and with beautiful eyes and handsome, God said to Samuel, "This is my choice; this is the lad who will be king" (1 Sam. 16:1-13).

Saul meets David

So this great destiny was laid on David. Soon he was to be introduced into the presence of Saul. There had come into Saul's mind an evil sickness and a kind of spasmodic madness; and when these attacks came upon him the only thing that would soothe his troubled mind was music. Now the young David was a skilful player upon the harp and he was introduced to Saul so that when the black fit came upon him David might play and bring back peace to his mind (1 Sam. 16:14-18). At first Saul loved David and he made him his armour-bearer. At first it looked as if the relationship between the two was going to be close and dear.

A mighty Exploit

But soon David was to begin his heroic deeds. At that time the great enemies of the Israelites were the Philistines and in their ranks they had a giant of a man called Goliath whose strength and prowess had struck terror into the hearts of the Israelites, paralysing them into helpless inaction. Now David's seven brothers were with Saul's army and David was sent down to them with some extra supplies and provisions. When he arrived he found the whole army scared of Goliath. To the incredulous amazement, and indeed the irritated anger of his brothers, David offered to take on this Philistine champion. He was brought before Saul and Saul was amazed that one so young should attempt such a task. David, however, answered, "Young I may be, but already as I kept the flock, I have killed a lion and a bear with my own bare hands." So Saul equipped David with full armour, but after David had tried it on he would have none of it. All he wanted was his shepherd's sling and five smooth pebbles from the brook; and with his sling he challenged the Philistine champion and slew him and delivered his countrymen from their terror (1 Sam. 17).

The Beginning of Jealousy

So David went from strength to strength until the whole country rang with the tale of his gallant exploits against the Philistines. As he came home one day from one of his sallies against the Philistines Saul was there. The singing women came out to greet the conqueror and the song they sang was: "Saul has slain his thousands, and David his ten thousands." And immediately there rose in Saul's heart a black tide of jealousy for the honour in which David was held (1 Sam. 18:5-9).

Saul seeks David's Life

From that time David's life was never safe. As he played his harp before Saul, Saul took his spear and hurled it at him, seeking to murder him (1 Sam. 18:10, 11). One of David's greatest friends, a man whom he loved more than a brother, was Jonathan, Saul's son. Jonathan did all he could to persuade Saul not to persist in this murderous hatred of David, but it was all to no avail. Not even in his own house was David safe. He was married to Michal, Saul's daughter. Saul's emissaries came to David's house to kill him. But David escaped out of a window down the wall and Michal created a dummy figure in the bed to make it seem that David was lying there ill, and so David made his escape. There was no appeasing Saul (1 Sam. 19:8-17). There came a day when David was due to sit at meat with Saul; but he feared to do so, for he knew that Saul was out for his life. So he made a plan with Jonathan. Jonathan was to see how Saul's mind was. David was to hide in a field. Jonathan would come out and shoot three arrows as if he was practising archery. When his lad ran to fetch the arrows if Jonathan called out that they were on this side of him all was well; if he called that they were beyond, then David's life was in danger. So the plan was carried out. Jonathan discovered that his father was still hot for the blood of David so he shot his arrows and called to the lad who went to fetch them that they were beyond and David knew that his life was still in danger (1 Sam. 20).

The Exile and Outlaw

For a time David became an exile and an outlaw. He took shelter with the Philistines; but they, too, suspected him and he could only gain safety by pretending to be mad (1 Sam. 21:10-15). He even took his father and mother and brought them over to Moab lest they, too, should be caught up in his perils and suffer in his danger (1 Sam. 22:3, 4). And then there came a time which for David was a terrible time. We catch glimpses of him in the cave of Adullam with 400 men as desperate as himself (1 Sam. 22:1, 2): in the wilderness of Ziph while Saul sought him every day (1 Sam. 23:14): in the oasis of Engedi down by the Dead Sea (1 Sam. 23:29). It was in Engedi that David showed his greatness. Saul had gone into a cave and David and his men, all unbeknown to Saul, were already there. David could have killed Saul on the spot. But instead, without Saul even knowing that it had happened, he cut off the skirt of Saul's robe and then confronted Saul with what he had done (1 Sam. 24). For a while such magnanimity reconciled even Saul; but the demon of jealousy would not be stilled. Once again David was in the wilderness, this time near Jeshimmon, which means the Devastation; Saul had come after him with three thousand men. In the dead of night David with Abishai stole into Saul's very tent and again David could have put an end to Saul and all his troubles; from Saul's pillow he took the jar of water and from his side he took his spear; and once again when Saul saw how David had spared his life his heart smote him; but once more jealousy conquered (1 Sam. 26). It was after that that David took what for him must have been the bitterest step of all, for he took service with the Philistines, the ancestral enemies of his country. He was safer with his enemies than he was with his own king.

The End for Saul

But Saul's days were numbered now. In the battle of Gilboa he was heavily defeated and in the end he took his own life

(1 Sam. 31:1-6). To David there came an Amalekite youth who claimed to have slain Saul. He brought to David the royal crown and the royal bracelet which he claimed to have taken from Saul's body. He expected to be praised and thanked, but David ordered him to be killed because he had raised his hand against the Lord's anointed, a thing David himself had never done although he had chance after chance to do so (2 Sam. 1:1-16). So David at last had peace from his enemies and ruled as king. At first things went well with him. He reigned in Hebron for seven and a half years. But David knew well that he could never really be master of Judaea until he had control of Jerusalem which at that time belonged to the Jebusites. So he attacked it. The inhabitants laughed at him. They declared that an army of cripples could hold the city against David's forces; but David stormed it and took it and Jerusalem became forever after the capital of Judaea and the city of David (2 Sam. 5:1-10).

The Troubles of David

For a time things went well with David. He extended the kingdom of Israel beyond the widest boundaries it had ever had. Moab, Syria, Edom, Ammon, even Damascus were under his sway (2 Sam. 8). But then life for David began to go wrong. To begin with David committed sin. He fell in love with Bath-sheba, but Bath-sheba was the wife of Uriah. So David did an ugly thing. He pretended to honour Uriah, but Uriah was a soldier and David sent secret orders to Joab, his commander-in-chief, telling him to place Uriah in such a position in battle that he was bound to be killed and Joab did so and Bath-sheba was taken by David (2 Sam. 11). But fortunately for David's soul there was a prophet with the word of God on his lips and the courage of God in his heart. His name was Nathan. He told David a story of a rich man who had everything and who despoiled a poor man of the one ewe lamb that he possessed. David's generous heart was kindled. He demanded the man's name that he might suffer for his selfishness and his arrogant and pitiless conduct; and back came Nathan's answer, "You are the man" (2 Sam. 12:1-14). But there was worse to come. David had a son called Absalom. He was disloyal to David. He was a handsome young man with all the charm in the world and, with specious and flattering words, he stole away the hearts of the people (2 Sam. 14:25 to 15:11). In the end David had to flee the country. After a time David won his country back again but for him the bloom was off the victory because Absalom was slain (2 Sam. 18).

The Death of David

For thirty-three years David reigned; and then full of years and honour he came to the end. He called his son Solomon and gave him his last words, "I am about to go the way of all the earth. Be strong and show yourself a man, and keep the charge of the Lord your God, walking in his ways and keeping his statutes and his commandments" (1 Kings 2:1-3). David had had a hard life, but he had found Israel a collection of tribes and had left her a strong nation with the city of David to be her capital.

QUESTIONS FOR DISCUSSION

Read 2 Samuel, chapters 11 and 12, and then discuss the following:

1. How could a man like David treat Uriah as he did?

2. How could he be so blind as not to see the meaning of Nathan's parable?

3. David, the man who sinned and repented.

3. DAVID, THE MAN AND HIS CHARACTER

The Man of Courage

Now that we have seen the kind of life that David lived, we must look at the man himself, so that we may see the qualities which made him so great a king and so important a person in the working out of the purpose and the plan of God. First and foremost, *David was a man of courage*. When Saul doubted if

David was strong enough to face the vast Goliath, David told how, when he was shepherding the flock, with his own bare hands, he killed a lion and a bear which had attacked the flock (1 Sam. 17:34-36). In Judaea a shepherd had to be a brave man. Judaea was a hard country. Up the centre of the country there ran a narrow rocky moorland plateau. It was never more than 15 miles across from west to east. On the west side there lay, running down to the sea, a region called the Shephelah, a region of hills with rocks and crannies and gulleys; on the east side it was worse, for on the east was one of the most terrible deserts in the world, a place of bare, bleak, sunbaked rocks and crags ending in the precipices which fell sheer 1,800 feet down to the Dead Sea. There was no fencing and no dykes or walls. Therefore the shepherd had to be on constant watch; and often when the sheep strayed away he had to take his life in his hands amongst the caves and rocks and precipices to find the sheep that was lost. Further, in the time of David, there were wild and savage beasts there ever ready to attack the flock. Sir George Adam Smith who travelled in Palestine describes the shepherds he saw: "On some high moor, across which at night the hyenas howl, when you meet him, sleepless, far-sighted, weather-beaten, armed, leaning on his staff, and looking out over his scattered sheep, every one on his heart, you understand why the shepherd of Judaea sprang to the front in his people's history." David was trained in a hard school. He needed the fittest of bodies and the bravest of hearts to be a shepherd. To begin with, David was a man of courage who must have been used to taking his life in his hands for his sheep.

The born Leader

Still further, David was *a born leader of men*. In our own experience we know how some people can get the best out of others; how they can bring out the extra effort; just how they can command that extra loyalty; some people are born to be captains. David was like that. His own men loved him. Once, in the days of his trouble, he was lying in the cave of Adullam. Suddenly there came to him a great desire. "If only," he said,

"I could get a drink of water from the well of Bethlehem that is by the gate." Three of his mighty men heard him. Bethlehem was 15 miles away and between it and them there lay their enemies, but down to Bethlehem they went and drew the water and brought it back to the leader they loved. And when they came back David would not drink it because he said that it was more than water; it was the very lives of these men, and so he poured it out as an offering to God (2 Sam. 23:13-17). That is the kind of thing men would do for David.

When Absalom turned against David and when David's fortunes were at their lowest ebb and when he was fleeing for his life he called one of his captains to him. The man's name was Ittai; he was not an Israelite at all; he was a Gittite. He was a soldier of fortune who would sell his sword to the highest bidder. David said to him, "There is no call for you to be mixed up in my misfortunes. Make your escape while there is time, and God's blessing be with you." And Ittai answered, "As the Lord lives, and as my lord the king lives, wherever my lord the king shall be, whether for death or for life, there also will your servant be" (2 Sam. 15:19-22). That is the kind of loyalty that David could command.

When the last struggle was on and when once again David wished to lead his men into battle his people would not let him go. "You shall not go out," they said, "for you are worth ten thousand of us" (2 Sam. 18:3). David was too dear to his people for them to let him risk death in his old age.

Whence came this love and loyalty? It came from this, that David never demanded that his men should face what he would not face himself. There is a famous story from Roman history. The great general Fabius Cunctator was faced with a difficult situation. A certain enemy stronghold stood in his way. One of his staff said, "Let it be stormed. It will only cost a few lives to take it." Fabius answered him, "Are *you* ready to be one of the few?" David was always ready to run the risks his men ran and so they loved him. People always respect a man who will never ask anyone else to do what he is not prepared to do himself.

The Man who made his Mistakes and accepted his Corrections

David was no plaster saint. David made mistakes and terrible mistakes. The worst thing he ever did was to fall in love with Bath-sheba who was Uriah's wife and then arrange that Uriah should be put in such a place in the battle that he was bound to be killed (2 Sam. 11). When Nathan the prophet heard that, he rebuked David in a stern story. David admitted his sin and repented (2 Sam. 12:1-13). Any man can sin; that is too fatally easy. But it takes a big man to accept a rebuke and to admit that he was wrong and to say publicly that he was sorry. Dr. Johnson became one of the greatest literary figures in England, a man whom everyone respected and admired. Dr. Johnson's father had been a poor man who had once owned a secondhand bookstall in the market place at Lichfield. Once he asked Johnson to look after it for an afternoon and Johnson was too proud to do so. Years later, when he was great and famous, he remembered; and he went and stood bareheaded in the rain for an hour in the market place at Lichfield to admit that he had been wrong and to show that he was sorry. There is none of us who can wholly avoid making mistakes. That is nothing to be ashamed of. But we ought to be thoroughly ashamed if we cannot accept a rebuke, if we cannot admit that we were wrong, and if we cannot say that we are sorry.

The Man who could forgive

Very specially David was *the man who could forgive*. In the days of his misfortune, when he was going into exile apparently a broken man, there came a man called Shimei and this man took advantage of the king's misfortune to vent his spleen upon him. He called David names, he cursed him, he even pursued him along the road with curses and he flung stones at him. Shimei was that most loathsome of creatures— one who kicked a man when he was down (2 Sam. 16:5-14). The day came when the tables were turned and when David returned in triumph. And then Shimei came crawling abjectly for forgiveness. David's captains would have slaughtered him— and who shall blame them? But David's answer was that not a man should be put to death that day in Israel and that he freely forgave (2 Sam. 19:16-23). All through life it is much easier to bear a grudge than it is to forget; it is much easier to take vengeance when we can than to forgive. Anyone can do that. It takes a really big man to forgive. And in this—as in all things—Jesus is our example. Once Paul wrote to his friends, "Be kind to one another, tenderhearted, forgiving one another, as God in Christ has forgiven you" (Eph. 4:32). David was like that; and we must be like that too.

The Man of Gratitude

But if David could forget an insult he never could forget a kindness done to him. He was supremely *the man of gratitude*. David's great friend had been Jonathan, Saul's son. When David came to the throne he asked if there were any of Saul's descendants left alive so that he might be kind to them. Jonathan's son Mephibosheth was still alive. In those days it would have been the natural thing to slaughter Mephibosheth. Kings were never secure upon their throne and it was just around a son of the previous king or a relative of his that rebellion and revolution could gather. But David never thought of that; all he remembered was that Jonathan had been kind to him and he must repay the debt (2 Sam. 9).

There is a famous Irish family which has the strangest coat of arms. It is the figure of a monkey and beneath it is the motto, "I will not forget what he did for me." Centuries before, the head of the family had had to leave home. He had to leave behind him his little baby son. He gave the sternest instructions for the baby's safekeeping. A fire broke out in the castle and the servants selfishly forgot all about the baby and saved themselves. It seemed that the helpless little child would be burned to death. In the castle there was a pet monkey. All of a sudden they saw the monkey on the battlements of the castle with the baby in its arms; at first they were terrified; but monkeys can climb and down the wall came the monkey holding the little baby and so saved the life of the heir. When the master came home he dealt sternly with the servants but he took as his crest a monkey with a baby in its arms and as a motto the words, "I will not forget what he did for me." David never forgot what a friend had done for him. Ingratitude is the ugliest of all sins. We, too, must be like David and never forget the things that others have done for us.

The Man of God

But above all else, *David was a man of God*. He could make his mistakes, he could do his wrong things; but always at the back of his mind there was God. That is why he was great. David was so great a captain and a king because he himself was the soldier and servant of God. If we will remember and never forget that we are living ever in our great taskmaster's eye we, too, will make something worth while out of life.

David the King

David was the man of courage; the man of leadership; the man who could make mistakes and accept correction; the man of forgiveness; the man of gratitude; the man of God. He was a man after God's own heart.

QUESTIONS FOR DISCUSSION

1. Using David as an example, work out what the qualities of leadership are.

2. What made people specially love David?

3. What would you say David's weaknesses were?

4. SOLOMON, WISDOM AND FOLLY

Solomon comes to the Throne

Of all the kings of Israel Solomon is the strangest mixture. It is true to say that he was one of the greatest of the kings; and yet it was in his reign that there were sown the seeds which were to result in the complete break-up of the kingdom. It is true to say that he was one of the wisest of men; and yet it is also true to say that he was guilty of the most ruinous folly.

David had many wives and many sons, but the son he chose as his successor on the throne was Solomon, the son of Bath-sheba. It was a widely extending kingdom which Solomon inherited, for David had made his influence felt as far away as Damascus (2 Sam. 8:6). It was almost in a bath of blood that Solomon came to the throne. David was old and in his old age he was no longer fit to govern the kingdom. When David was failing mentally and physically another and older of his sons called Adonijah tried to insinuate himself into the power. He was the son of a woman called Haggith (1 Kings 1:5). He was a handsome and an attractive person and it seemed that he might well steal away the hearts of the people (1 Kings 1:6). He had, in fact, seduced from their loyalty two of the king's greatest men, Joab, the commander-in-chief of the army and Abiathar, the High Priest (1 Kings 1:7). Seeing the danger, Bath-sheba, Solomon's mother, persuaded the aged David to act and to nominate Solomon as his successor (1 Kings 1:11-40). So David died and Solomon ascended the throne and he acted with savage vigour. First of all Adonijah was murdered (1 Kings 2:19-25). Then Abiathar the High Priest was dismissed from office (1 Kings 2:26, 27). When Joab heard of this he took refuge in the tabernacle beside the altar where he should have been immune from death; but Solomon sent his messengers and murdered him, too (1 Kings 2:28-34). Solomon had dealt with his rivals in the sternest and the most terrible way. And a man cannot enter upon a kingdom like that without leaving a trail of broken and resentful hearts behind him.

Solomon's Dream

In spite of this savage work Solomon began well. He had a dream in which God came to him and offered to give him any gift that he might desire. Solomon did not ask for wealth or greatness or power; he asked for the understanding heart (1 Kings 3:5-15). It was as a wise man that Solomon was forever famous. There were many legends about him. The legends tell that he could understand the language of the birds and of the beasts and that he never needed to examine any witness when he was trying a case because he could read what was in a man's heart simply by looking at him. In 1 Kings 3:16-18 we have an example of Solomon's practical wisdom in judgment. There were two women who lived in the same house and both had little babies. In the night, as she slept, one of them lay on the top of her little baby and so smothered it. When she saw what she had done she rose and, while the other slept, she stole the living baby away and put her dead one beside her. The one whose child had been so stolen woke in the morning and found a dead child with her. She knew the dead child was not hers; and she knew that the other woman had stolen her child; but the other woman would not give up the child she had stolen. So the case was taken to Solomon. Solomon made his decision at once. He said, "Let the child be cut in two and half the child given to each woman." One of the women agreed at once to this solution. The other said, "No; rather than that give the child to her; rather that than see him dead." And Solomon knew at once that the woman who agreed that the child should be cut up was the woman who had stolen the child. The woman who would agree to the child being given away rather than that he should be killed must be the mother, because a mother would never agree to the death of her child and would do anything to save his life. And Solomon was right. There were times when Solomon was wise in his judgments of people.

Solomon the Builder

Solomon had a passion for building. First of all he decided to build a Temple in Jerusalem where men might worship God. To that end he needed cedar trees from Lebanon and he entered into an agreement with Hiram, king of Tyre, to get them. But Solomon needed men to hew down the trees and so he raised a levy of forced labour. He took 30,000 men and he sent them to Lebanon 10,000 at a time, so that each of these men was two months at home and a month away in Lebanon; he had 70,000 burden bearers and 80,000 hewers of wood. The Temple was seven years in building. 1 Kings 6 tells the story of the building. Now this levy could not cause anything else but trouble. No man likes to be taken away from his home and from his family; and Solomon must have caused the gravest discontent and unrest amongst his people by making his people do this work, even although it was to build the Temple. Second, he began to build his own palace (1 Kings 7). It was thirteen years in building and once again the people who were forced to labour on it must have resented the tasks that were forced upon them. Third, Solomon was a great builder of cities (2 Chron. 8:1-6). So still more people must have been involved in forced labour and must have been restive and unhappy. Solomon was certainly raising immense and wonderful buildings, but he was also building up a legacy of trouble which some day someone was going to inherit.

The Luxury of Solomon

Still further, no one ever lived in such luxury as Solomon did. He taxed the people heavily. He had twelve officers over the kingdom whose job it was to provide victuals for the king's household (1 Kings 4:7). 1 Kings 4:22, 23 tells us what the provision for *one day* was—"Thirty cors of fine flour, and sixty cors of meal, ten fat oxen, and twenty pasture-fed cattle, a hundred sheep, besides harts, gazelles, roebucks and fatted fowl." Someone had to supply all this and we read of Solomon raising levies (e.g. 1 Kings 9:15). We read of him living in a luxury that David the shepherd king could never have dreamed of. Even his drinking vessels were of gold (1 Kings 10:31). He had a throne of ivory and gold that was one of the wonders of the world (1 Kings 10:18-20). Silver was of no account in the days of Solomon (1 Kings 10:21); silver was as plentiful as stones and cedars as sycamores (1 Kings 10:27; 2 Chron. 1:15). Again all this must have cost money; someone had to to pay for it; the only way in which it could be paid for was by taxing the people. Beneath the surface there was a seething discontent which in the end was to ruin the country forever.

Solomon's Foreign Policy

But if Solomon's conduct of home affairs was piling up trouble his foreign policy was in the end calculated to be even more disastrous. It had always been the deliberate policy of Israel that since they were God's own chosen people they must never entangle themselves in foreign alliances, but must have God as their only ally. But Solomon made his foreign alliances and they were doubly disastrous. He began with an alliance with Egypt (1 Kings 3:1). Now just here is the explanation of one of the strange things about Solomon. Even in the popular mind Solomon is known as the man who had many wives (1 Kings 11:1-7). We read of these strange and foreign wives and note the fact that many of them were princesses. There is a reason behind this. In ancient times when a treaty and an alliance was made between two countries one of the commonest ways of ratifying it was that one of the kings involved should marry the daughter of the other. That set the seal upon the agreement. That is the explanation of Solomon's harem. Whenever Solomon made another foreign alliance he contracted another marriage with a foreign princess. That was bad enough, but what made it worse was this. In those old days most people believed that every country had its own god; and for the people of that country that was the only god. They never denied that the other gods were real; they only said that for them there was only one god, the god of their own country; other peoples of other countries had other gods which were just as real. So then whenever Solomon took another foreign princess into his palace she brought with her the worship of another strange god; and so the purity of Solomon's religion was tainted and he began to worship all kinds of gods. The tragedy was that Solomon's foreign alliances ruined the clean purity of the Israelites' faith in the true God. Once again there was infinite cause for trouble here.

The Death of Solomon

So for forty years Solomon reigned in splendour and then he died bequeathing the kingdom to Rehoboam, his son; but with the kingdom he bequeathed to Rehoboam a legacy of trouble which was soon to destroy the kingdom.

The good Start and the bad Finish

Solomon was a man who began well and who finished badly. When he had his dream and when he chose wisdom above all things it looked as if here was a man who would make a real success of life and of kingship, but he ended by straying after false and evil gods. In this life it is easy to start well; but it is not so easy to keep going well and in the end to finish well. Once there was a famous man and during his lifetime he was so famous that someone wanted to write his biography when he was still alive. He refused to allow it; he said, "I have seen too many men who fell out in the last lap of the race." Many men start fairly but never finish. Lord Fisher, the great sailor, used to say vividly, "Life is strewn with orange peel." There is nothing easier than to slip. In a race or game or in any activity of life the person who cannot stick it out is not much use. It is the player who can keep going to the last second of the game, the person who never lets up until the final goal is reached, who really succeeds in the end. One of the great problems of the Church is the number of people who start going to Church, but who do not keep it up. We must remember when things are hard and difficult and when we want to give up that Jesus is always with us and beside us; that we are not making this effort alone and that, if we ask him, he can keep us going even when we want to give up.

The King who was separate from his Subjects

The other bad thing about Solomon was this. David had been a man who lived with his people; he toiled with them, fought with them, laboured with them, lived with them. He shared their sorrows and their joys, their triumphs and their failures. But Solomon cut himself off from ordinary folk. He lived in his golden palace on his ivory throne in luxury. He forced his people to work and taxed them to keep him in splendour. David was one with the ordinary folk; Solomon was quite separated and cut off from them. That is why he was in the end not a good king. A real king shares his people's trials and troubles. There was a European king who often worried his government by going off in disguise and walking about in the humblest and the poorest places and talking to everybody he met. When they remonstrated with him he answered, "I cannot govern my people unless I know how they live." He wanted to be one with his people, not different from them. It is one of the outstanding facts that the countries where royalty still sits on the throne are countries where royalty is close to the people. In Denmark the king rode a bicycle through the streets like any other person. In our own country one of the things that endeared George the Sixth to his people was that he was one with them. When Buckingham Palace was hit by a bomb when the king was there, the people knew that the king was going through exactly the same as they were. It was true when they wrote of George the Sixth, "He gave himself even to the end". The true king is not separate from his people like Solomon, but one with them like David. That is what God was like. He did not stay away separate in heaven; he came to this earth in Jesus and lived our life and shared the troubles and the trials each one of us has.

QUESTIONS FOR DISCUSSION

1. Discuss the consequences of thinking politics more important than religion.

2. Wherein lies real national prosperity?

5. THE SPLIT IN THE KINGDOM

We have seen that Solomon's way of life and of governing was such that sooner or later it was bound to bring serious trouble. His passion for building made great forced levies of the people necessary and men are always discontented when they have to leave their homes and families for long periods to work practically as slaves. Both his building schemes and his way of life made high taxation necessary, and citizens always resent that. His luxury and his wealth and his riches removed him farther and farther from the ordinary man and inevitably there arose more grumbling than loyalty. Trouble was on the way. That trouble found a focus in Jeroboam. Jeroboam was young and efficient. He had been rapidly advanced in the government service; but it seems that people saw in him a champion of their rights whom they were prepared to follow (1 Kings 11:26-28).

Ahijah's dramatic Warning

All this came to a head in a dramatic action of the prophet Ahijah. In the old days the prophets had a custom which they often followed. When they desired to make something specially clear and vivid, when they desired to proclaim some truth in such a way that no one could possibly fail to see it, they made their announcement not in words, but in action. They put what they wanted to say into dramatic action. They did some arresting thing which was bound to compel people to see what they wanted to say. Now Ahijah knew that trouble was on the way. He knew that if Solomon went on as he was doing there could not fail to be a serious split in the kingdom. So Ahijah clad himself in a new robe. He went out and met Jeroboam all by himself. When he met Jeroboam he snatched off his robe and he deliberately tore it into twelve pieces. Of the twelve pieces he gave ten to Jeroboam and kept two. "That," said Ahijah, "is what is going to happen to this kingdom. It will be split from top to bottom and ten of the tribes will follow you; and only two will remain faithful to the house of David" (1 Kings 11:29-39). Obviously a thing like this would soon be known; and equally obviously a thing like this would deeply anger Solomon. Indeed it did; he sought to kill Jeroboam and Jeroboam had to take shelter in exile down in Egypt until his hour should come (1 Kings 11:40).

Rehoboam mounts the Throne

In due time Solomon died after reigning over the kingdom for forty years and his son Rehoboam came to the throne.

He went to Shechem to be crowned and Jeroboam's supporters
sent for him to come back from Egypt, and he came (1 Kings
12:1-3). The people saw in the new king their hope of release
from the burdens that Solomon had laid so long and so heavily
upon them. So they came to Rehoboam with a very reasonable
request. They said, "Your father Solomon made things very
difficult for us and laid very heavy burdens upon us; if you
will only make things a little easier for us we will gladly serve
you as king." Rehoboam said that he would take three days
to think it over. In the three days Rehoboam took counsel
with two sets of people. He consulted the older men and the
experienced statesmen. They advised him to meet the people
half way and to agree to make things easier for them. Then he
consulted the younger men who were his own contemporaries
and who had grown up with him. They advised him to say
that, so far from making things any easier, he proposed to
deal with them even more harshly than Solomon his father
and to lay even greater burdens upon them. Rehoboam
forsook the advice of the experienced statesmen and took
the advice of the younger men. He told the people that
his father had made their yoke heavy, but that he would
make it still heavier; that his father had chastised them with
whips, but that he would chastise them with scorpions (1 Kings
12:3-15).

The Split in the Kingdom

The consequence was disastrous, for then, as Ahijah had
foretold, ten tribes revolted and chose Jeroboam as their king
and only two remained faithful to Rehoboam (1 Kings 12:20).
At first Rehoboam wished to assemble his armies and to fight,
but he was warned by the prophet Shemaiah that it was hopeless
to go against the decree of God and so he could do no other
than accept the situation (1 Kings 12:21-24). The split in the
kingdom was a complete disaster. Geographically, the Israelites
were in a very dangerous position. They were a little nation and
they were between two great nations, for they were between
Syria in the north and Egypt in the south. So long as they were
united they had some chance of survival, but once they were

divided they were certain, sooner or later, to be swallowed up by their more powerful neighbours. So from this time on there are two kingdoms in Palestine. The one was called the Kingdom of Israel or the Northern Kingdom. Its capital was first at Shechem and later at Samaria. The other was called the Kingdom of Judah or the Southern Kingdom and its capital was at Jerusalem.

The whole business was a fatal mistake. The Jews were far too small a nation to split into two. This split happened in the year 962 B.C. More than nine hundred years later, in the time of Jesus, there were only about four and a half million Jews. There must have been many fewer then and a nation of that small size cannot afford to be split into disunity. Further, the land was far too small to divide. Very likely we do not realise how small Palestine is. From north to south it is less than 150 miles long and from east to west it varies from just over 20 miles to just over 40 miles wide. That is to say, from north to south Palestine is no longer than the journey from Perth to Carlisle, and from east to west it is not as long as the journey from Glasgow to Edinburgh. The whole of Palestine is only the size of Wales. The two resulting kingdoms were almost ridiculously small for independent kingdoms. Samaria was 40 miles from north to south and 35 miles from east to west. Judaea was 55 miles from north to south and from 25 to 35 miles from east to west, and a great part of Judaea was uninhabitable desert. The area of the Northern Kingdom was no more than 1,500 square miles and the area of the Southern Kingdom was no more than 2,000 square miles, of which only 1,400 square miles were inhabitable country. We may understand this better if we remember that Aberdeenshire is 1,955 square miles; Perthshire 2,528 square miles; Cumberland 1,516 square miles; Kent 1,515 square miles; and Devon 2,015 square miles. In other words there are many of our counties which are larger than either of the two kingdoms. It is clear to see, in face of this, what a total tragedy and disaster this split in the kingdom was; and it was a split which was never to be healed.

The Man who rejected the Verdict of Experience

Let us now look at the character of this man Rehoboam who effectively wrecked the united kingdom of Israel. First there stands out about him the fact that he was the man who did what no wise man will ever do—*he rejected the advice of experience.* When he asked the older and the wiser statesmen what he should do they advised him to accede to the request of the people and to make things easier for them; but Rehoboam rejected that advice. It is always hard for younger people to take the advice of those who are older. We are all apt to think that we know best and that older people are too careful and too cautious and too slow to move, and sometimes, indeed, they are. But we must remember this—that if we want advice and warning about the dangers and the pitfalls of any road, the best person to give it is a person who has walked that way before. If we are going on a motor car journey a map is a good thing, but still better is the advice of a man who has already driven the road that we intend to take. Older people have already travelled on the journey of life. When they give us advice we must be prepared at least to listen to it. We must try to remember that they do not only want to restrain us and control us and keep us down; they have been the road before and they know how dangerous life can be.

The Man who refused to right a Wrong

Further, Rehoboam did what no good men will ever do—*he refused to right a wrong when it was within his power to do so.* All through Solomon's reign the people had been oppressed, overworked and overtaxed. Rehoboam could easily have put all this to rights, but he refused to do so. There was a wrong and an injustice that it was within his power to right and he refused to right them. One of the most threatening parables Jesus ever spoke was the parable of the Rich Man and Lazarus (Luke 16:19-31). In that parable Jesus tells how there was a poor man called Lazarus who was daily cast down to beg at the gate of a rich man's house. The rich man was clothed in purple and fine linen and the poor man was so helpless that the dogs worried him and so poor that he was glad to get the bread that fell from the rich man's table. When both of these men died the poor man was taken up to the joys of heaven, but the rich man was condemned to the penalties and the pains of hell. Why was the rich man so terribly condemned? He was condemned because every day he passed Lazarus and did nothing to help him. He was not deliberately cruel to him. He did not order him to be removed; he did not kick him in the passing; he simply never noticed him. He accepted Lazarus as part of the landscape. He thought it quite natural and quite fitting that he should have far more than enough and Lazarus far less than too little. There was a man he might have helped and he did nothing about it and so he was condemned. If it is possible for us to right some wrong, to mend some injustice, to help someone in trouble and we refuse to do it—that is sin. Over and over again life will bring us chances to do something for someone and if we refuse these chances we will some day answer for our refusal.

The Man who never thought of the Future

Still further, Rehoboam did what no sensible man will ever do—*he never thought of the effect of his actions on the future*. He must have well known the simmering discontent that was among the people. If he had stopped to think he would have been bound to see how ruinous his policy of severity must be. But he never thought of the future at all. Louis the Sixteenth was King of France just before the Revolution. He was warned by his statesmen that unless he did something to alter things the revolution was bound to come. He used to say, "Keep things as they are so long as I am alive; after me let the deluge come." He was a man who disregarded the future and because of that the greatest troubles came both upon himself and upon his country.

The Epicureans used to insist that the aim and goal and end of life was pleasure. But they very carefully defined what they meant by pleasure. A thing might be hard and difficult and demanding at the present moment; it might even be painful and hurting; but if in the end it brought a deep satisfaction then it was true pleasure. On the other hand, a thing might be very pleasant and very delightful at the moment, but in the end it might bring regret and remorse, therefore it was not true pleasure. It is easier to play than to work; it is more pleasant at the moment to slack than to study; but in the end it is often the hard things which bring the real and the lasting pleasure. We must never be content to think only of how a thing seems at the moment. We must learn to take the long view of things if we wish to avoid trouble both for ourselves and for others.

The Man who split the Kingdom

Rehoboam goes down to history as the man who split the kingdom in two. He did what no wise man would ever do—he rejected the advice of experience. He did what no good man would ever do—he refused to right a wrong when it was within his power to do so. He did what no sensible man would ever do—he failed to think of the future effects of his action. Rehoboam is an example to us of how not to live.

QUESTIONS FOR DISCUSSION

1. What are the main reasons for the conflict between youth and age and experience? How can young people and older people learn to understand each other better?

2. What steps can we take to right wrongs?

3. How can we teach ourselves to take the long view of life?

6. ELIJAH, THE PROPHET OF GOD

(It is obviously impossible to trace the history of both the kingdoms in detail. All that we can do is to take one great representative figure from each of them. From the Northern Kingdom we choose the prophet Elijah.)

An evil King

About sixty years after the kingdom had split in two there came to the throne of the Northern Kingdom a king whose name has become a synonym for evil and for wickedness. His name was Ahab. Left to himself he might not have been so bad a man, but he married a princess whose name has passed into the English language as a description of a shameless and cruel wickedness. Her name was Jezebel and she was the daughter of Ethbaal, king of the Zidonians. When we were studying Solomon we saw that when a king made an alliance with another king the alliance was very often confirmed by a marriage with the foreign king's daughter; and we also saw that always these foreign princesses brought their foreign gods with them into the country. Jezebel brought with her the worship of the god Baal (1 Kings 16:29-33). She led away Ahab and many of the people to the worship of this god called Baal.

Baal Worship

When we read the Book of Kings and when we study the prophets we hear a great deal about Baal worship; so it is well that we should understand just what it was and what it involved. There were really a great many Baals. The word literally means Lord. The one thing that fascinated ancient peoples was the coming of life itself. Yearly they saw the harvest ripen; yearly they saw the grapes cover the vines and the olive trees grow; and they were fascinated at the thought of the power that every year brought about the growth and made the land fertile. They were also fascinated by the power that enabled children to be born. Now they believed the Baals to be the gods who made the corn grow and the grapes swell and the olives ripen and who were the power which enabled children to be born. The technical name for these Baals is fertility gods. The people worshipped these gods who, as they believed, gave them the harvest and gave them children. It was the way in which they worshipped them which was so dangerous. They believed that the way to worship these Baals was to use their gifts to the full. So at harvest time they glutted themselves with food and sated themselves with wine. They believed that by feasting gluttonously and becoming riotously drunk with wine they were worshipping the gods who gave the harvest. These Baals had their temples and their shrines. In these sacred places there were priestesses of Baal and these priestesses were sacred prostitutes; again the people believed that the way to worship the Baals was to behave in the most immoral way with these priestesses. The great and grave danger of the Baal worship was therefore twofold. It was a gluttonous, riotous, immoral worship, and it was just the kind of worship that would be extremely popular. It was so easy; it was so different from the clean, pure, austere worship of the true God. It appealed to the very things that men wanted to do and which the worship of the true God forbade. It was little wonder that the people were always in danger of being led away to Baal worship.

A Great Prophet arises

It was the great task of the prophets to combat this Baal worship. It was very difficult for the Israelites to escape the taint of it, because it was actually the religion of the Canaanites, who were the original people of the land and the infection of it was on every side. Now Jezebel brought this worship into the Northern Kingdom with her. Ahab accepted it; the people were seduced by it. Moral degeneration was on every side. Into this situation there strode the greatest of the prophets. His name was Elijah. He came from the village of Tishbeh, which was in Gilead, on the eastern side of the Jordan. Out of Gilead he burst on Ahab with a message of judgment. There was to be a drought which was to last for years and which was to bring famine on the kingdom. Thus would God punish the people for their wandering from him (1 Kings 17:1-3). Just as suddenly as he had come Elijah vanished into the wilds again, for Elijah came and went like some avenging spirit. But then Elijah decided to take another step and it was a step in which he took his life in his hands. He demanded that the prophets of the false gods should meet him at Carmel and that there, in the presence of the people, he and they should both try to bring down fire upon a sacrifice. All day long the frenzied prophets of Baal tried and failed; and then Elijah succeeded (1 Kings 18:1-39). That was bad enough; but after their discomfiture, Elijah had every one of these false prophets slaughtered (1 Kings 18:40). Elijah must well have known that from that moment Jezebel would be his implacable enemy, but there are times when only surgical means can remove a cancerous growth from the body and there are times in a country when evil must of necessity be destroyed. And then after more than two years of drought, there came the rain and the land was saved from its famine (1 Kings 18:41-46). It seemed that God's mercy was going out to the penitent land.

A Prophet's Hour of Reaction

Then the hour of reaction came to Elijah. A prophet is necessarily a man of intense nature and inevitably he must know the extremes of hope and despair. Jezebel was vowing vengeance and Elijah fled to the desert beyond Beersheba. Carmel is almost in the extreme north of Palestine; Beersheba is the farthest south town before the desert begins. Elijah in his moment of reaction put the whole length of the country between himself and the enraged queen. But out in the desert, in the lonely mount of Horeb, a hundred and seventy miles farther on than Beersheba, God met Elijah and Elijah's faith came back. Elijah did what only a wise man would do. In the hour when all men were against him he sought God and God gave him back his strength and courage (1 Kings 19:1-18).

A Tyrant defied

But Elijah's exploits were not finished. There was a man in Samaria called Naboth. His little patch of ground was next the ground of Ahab and Ahab desired to have it. Naboth refused to part with it, as indeed he was bound to refuse for the law laid it down that a man might only sell his ground to a kinsman (Lev. 25:23; Num. 36:7). Ahab was ill with disappointment. Jezebel found out the cause of his illness; she took matters into her own hands; she arranged the murder of Naboth, and Ahab entered into possession of the ground he had coveted. Ahab went down to the ground to enjoy it and like a bolt from the blue Elijah burst upon the scene and pronounced God's judgment on him. If ever a man took his life in his hands Elijah did so that day (1 Kings 21:1-26). So Elijah continued to witness to truth and righteousness until the day when he handed over his lifework to Elisha and God took him to himself (2 Kings 2:1-11).

The Man with a fearless Message

The Jews have always regarded Elijah as the greatest of the prophets. Let us look at the characteristics of this heroic figure. For one thing, *Elijah was a man who did not hesitate to tell the truth, even when the truth was bad news*. Right at the beginning he came to Ahab with tidings of the drought which was to come. That was bad news. It was always dangerous to bring bad news to an eastern despot; for a despotic king might very well execute the man who dared to bring bad news to him. However unpleasant the truth might be, Elijah told it. Once Melville, the great Scottish forerunner of the Reformation, made some true but dangerous statements about the king. They told him that if he said things like that he would certainly be executed. "Is what I said true?" he asked. They told him, "Yes, it is true." "Then," said Melville, "if it is true let it stand." He did not seek safety, he sought truth. People who tell the truth often suffer for it because people seldom like to hear unpleasant things. Jesus himself said to his enemies, "Now you seek to kill me, a man who has told you the truth" (John 8:40). The way of truth is not an easy way; but it is better to suffer with the truth than to avoid trouble with a lie.

The Man who saw the Danger of Compromise

Elijah was *the man who would have nothing to do with compromise*. It was not that the people of Israel desired completely to abandon the true God; it was that they wanted to worship God *and* Baal; and Elijah saw quite clearly that it could not be done. His question to the people was, "How long will you go limping with two different opinions?" (1 Kings 18:21). Always in life we have got to be on one side or the other. There is a story of Faraday, the famous scientist. When he was young he had to make his living by taking round the daily papers. Newspapers in those days were only printed in small numbers; and at each house he had to wait until the person read the paper and then he had to take it on to the next. While he was waiting at one house he was experimenting with putting his head through the railings of the house. He got his head through and then discovered that he could not get it back again. He was not a bit afraid for even then he had the scientific temperament! In his mind there was a question: "My head is on one side of the railings; my body is on the other; *on which side am I*?" That is exactly the question that every one of us must ask and answer. We can never serve two masters. There is no room for compromise in the Christian life. With God it is a case of all or nothing. There is only one place for God and that is first in our lives.

The Man who defied the Tyrant

Elijah was *the man who was ready to risk his life to defy a tyrant*. When Ahab stole Naboth's vineyard by having Naboth murdered at Jezebel's instigation only Elijah had the courage to tell him exactly what he had done. It is the simple truth that we owe our liberty and all our most cherished rights and freedoms to men who were prepared to risk their lives in order to face tyrants who sought to destroy liberty. Charles the First was in a fair way to take from this country the liberties that all men cherished. Certain men took a stand against them. In particular there were five members of Parliament who stood for freedom. He came into Parliament. He demanded that Parliament should either immediately hand these men over or should tell him where they were to be found. He demanded that Lenthall, the Speaker of the House of Commons, should point them out to him. "Sir," said Lenthall, "I have neither eyes to see nor tongue to say anything except what this House commands me." When he said that he risked his life to maintain the freedom and the liberty of the House of Commons and of the country. Sometimes in life we will have the opportunity to stand against either a tyrant or a bully. It is never our rights that we should be so eager to protect but the rights of others. The person who risks his own safety and comfort and security for the sake of the rights of someone who is weaker and less able to defend himself is always doing a fine and a Christian thing.

The heroic Prophet

Elijah was the man who did not hesitate to tell the truth even when the truth was bad news; he was the man who would have nothing to do with compromise; he was the man who was ready to risk his life to defy a tyrant for the sake of someone who was not able to defend himself. Elijah was the man who held Israel on the right road when the nation was likely to go astray.

QUESTIONS FOR DISCUSSION

1. There are different ways of speaking the truth. Paul speaks of speaking the truth in love (Eph. 4:15). What ways of speaking the truth are most effective, and what ways least effective?

2. When is it right, and when is it wrong, to compromise?

3. When is it right, and when is it wrong, to defy authority?

7. THE END OF A KINGDOM

The Terrible Years

It was in 962 B.C. that there came the split in the kingdom which was never healed; and it was in 721 B.C., rather more than 240 years later, that Samaria fell to the Assyrians and the Northern Kindom perished forever. It is at that final destruction that we must now look. We have seen how Elijah struggled and risked his life to try to keep his countrymen true to God. That was the struggle of all the prophets, but it was a never-ending and a losing struggle for time and time again the people were disobedient and strayed away from God. We cannot trace the history of the whole period but we must look at the last terrible years. The 17 years from 738 B.C. to 721 B.C. were a crescendo of disaster and of trouble. Throughout these years it must have been clear to anyone who could read the signs of the times that an avalanche of trouble was crashing down upon the Northern Kingdom.

The Beginning of the End

We have already seen how small a land Palestine was and how comparatively few were its inhabitants. The great problem of Palestine was that it lay between two mighty empires. To the north-east lay Assyria, one of the greatest empires in the world; to the south there lay Egypt, another of the world's great powers. Inevitably every now and then these great empires were filled with thoughts and schemes of world dominion and inevitably the first step on their projected pathway to power was Palestine. By its very geographical position Palestine was always liable to be crushed between the upper and the nether millstones of the great empires. In 738 B.C. the first warnings of the end came. At that time a king called Menahem reigned in Samaria and Assyria was on the march. The name of the Assyrian king was Tiglath-pileser. He was threatening to engulf the Northern Kingdom and obviously there was no hope in armed resistance for no army that Samaria could ever put in the field could hope to stop the Assyrians. Menahem did the only thing possible. He bought his safety. He gave the Assyrian king one thousand talents of silver. A silver talent was worth about £240. So the little kingdom of Samaria had to buy its way to safety at a price of almost a quarter of a million pounds. Menahem raised the money by a forced levy on the wealthier classes. But the trouble was there. A bribe can never effectively buy safety; the blackmailer will always come back for more; Menahem's kingdom was now under constant threat from without and, beyond a doubt, such a levy must have raised constant discontent within. The end is now in sight (2 Kings 15:17-20).

The gathering Storm

Now the pace begins to accelerate and the Northern Kingdom began not only to be in peril from without but also to disrupt from within. Menahem was succeeded by his son Pekahiah who reigned for two years and was then murdered by one of his own captains called Pekah (2 Kings 15:22-26). Pekah gained the throne, but he gained trouble too. For very soon Tiglath-pileser of Assyria descended upon the Northern Kingdom again and this time did not stop until he had captured the greater part of Galilee and the country north of that and had carried away the inhabitants captive to Assyria. The net was closing in (2 Kings 15:27-29).

The End comes

The end was now hastening on. It was by murder that Pekah came to the throne and it was by murder he left it; for he himself was murdered by Hoshea (2 Kings 15:30). By this time Tiglath-pileser was dead, but his successor, Shalmaneser, descended once again on the Northern Kingdom. At first Hoshea was able to buy him off by giving him tribute. But Hoshea began to play a dangerous game and in the end it ruined him. We have already seen that Palestine was between two great countries. On the north there was Assyria and to the south there lay Egypt. Hoshea tried a desperate remedy. He was pressed by Assyria and he tried to wriggle out of the situation by engineering a treaty with Egypt. Doubtless he desired to play off one great empire against the other. Shalmaneser discovered the plan and struck. Samaria itself was besieged. For three years it held out, but in 721 B.C. the end came. Shalmaneser was thorough. He carried the best of the people, more than 20,000 of them, away into captivity in Assyria. The Northern Kingdom was not only conquered; it was obliterated; and it passed from history forever. The mad 17 years from 738 B.C. to 721 B.C. had come to an end and the end was that the Northern Kingdom was wiped out forever, and foreigners from far countries were brought in to dwell in the land which had once belonged to Israel.

The wrong Things Men did

The Bible always shows that nothing happens by accident and by chance, but that everything is working out the plan and the purpose of God. So then the writer of 2 Kings believed that there was a reason for this disaster that had fallen on the Northern Kingdom, and that God was behind even this. So in a very interesting passage (2 Kings 17:6-23) he gives what he believes to be the reasons why all this came upon the Northern Kingdom.

Forgetting God's Benefits

First of all, disaster came upon the Northern Kingdom because *they forgot God's benefits*. They forgot what God had done for them. It was God who had brought them up from the land of Egypt from under the hand of Pharaoh (2 Kings 17:7). Long ago they had been slaves in the land of Egypt with the lash of the taskmaster laid upon their backs and with their freedom gone. It was God who had rescued them from slavery, who had led them through the desert, who had brought them into the Promised Land and who had made them a great people—and now they had forgotten all about it. Of all things ingratitude is the ugliest, and of all things it is the most hurting. In Shakespeare's play, *King Lear*, Lear's daughters turned against him in his old age after he had done everything possible for them; and then the old king said:

> "How sharper than a serpent's tooth it is
> To have a thankless child."

We so often deal with God in a very shameful way. When we want God we remember him. If we are afraid, or if we have something very difficult to do, or if we are in danger, or if someone we love is in danger, then we remember to pray to God; but if things are going well and life is easy and the sun is shining, then we forget all about God. We have a duty that sometimes we should sit down and think of all the gifts we have which come to us from God, things that we could never have made or gained for ourselves but which God gave us. There is the world we live in, the food we eat, the health we enjoy, the ability to see and to hear and to walk and to run; there are our minds and our ability to think and to learn and to remember; there is life itself; and, above all, there is Jesus. If we sat down to make a list and if we headed it "The things I owe to God," it would be a list that we could never finish. We must never forget what we owe to God. It we try always to remember it will keep us grateful and it will keep us true.

Disobeying God's Commandments

Further, disaster came upon the Northern Kingdom because *they disobeyed God's commandments*. They did the things "of which the Lord had said unto them, 'You shall not do this'" (2 Kings 17:12). In every department of life we must obey the rules. If we are ever to learn and to become wise, we must obey the rules of school and college. If we are ever to be well and healthy, we must obey the rules of health. When we play games, the game is ruined unless we play it according to the rules. Diogenes, a famous Greek philosopher, once said that he just could not understand men. They went to the dentist, the oculist, the doctor; and they did what these experts told them to do; but they never went to God and did what he told them to do that their souls might be healthy as well as their bodies. God's commandments to us must be right because of two things. First, only God really knows what is for our good. When we are very young we want to do things and to eat things and so on which our parents know are harmful to us; and very wisely they will not let us do these things. We do not know any better. We are like that all our lives with God; only he is wise enough to know what is for our good. Secondly, only God can foresee the future. We cannot tell what is going to happen at the end of today, let alone some years hence. And so often we want to do things which in the end would only hurt and harm us. But God foresees and God knows. Therefore his commandments must be good. There is just one rule always to observe—if we always ask in every situation and in every moment of the day, "Lord, what do *you* want me to do?" life will never come to disaster for us as it did for these Israelites long ago.

Disregarding God's Messengers

Still further, disaster came upon the Northern Kingdom because *they disregarded God's messengers*. God sent them messages again and again by the prophets, but they disregarded the messages and went their own way (2 Kings 17:13). In the North of England the county authorities were repairing a certain stretch of road. It was a dangerous bit of road because there was, first of all, a sharp bend and then a narrow bridge and then another sharp bend and half the road was up. A good distance before it there were signs telling the motorists to be careful. And then just immediately before it there was this sign in huge letters: YOU HAVE BEEN WARNED. This said to the drivers who used that road, "If you disregard all the signs and if you drive on carelessly and recklessly and if you have a smash and injure yourself, you have nobody to blame but yourself because every possible warning has been given to you." Life is like that. We have all kinds of things which warn us when we are going to do wrong. We have God's book to tell us what to do; we have our Church to teach us and train us in the right way; we have our parents and those who are older and wiser than we are to give us good advice; we have our consciences to tell us when we are doing wrong; we have the presence of Jesus always with us. We never lack for messengers from God to tell us what is right and what is wrong, what is our duty and what we must avoid. We, too, have been warned; and anyone who does not take a warning is a very foolish person and has no one but himself to blame if trouble comes upon him.

Worshipping God in the wrong Way

Lastly, in consequence of their forgetfulness, their disobedience and their disregard, disaster came upon the Northern Kingdom because *they worshipped God in the wrong way* (2 Kings 17:16, 17). They worshipped idols; they used all kinds of superstitions and magic things. It says one terrible thing—"they made their sons and daughters pass through the fire." That means that they actually thought that they were pleasing God by sacrificing and burning babies in the fire. There is one very terrible verse in 1 Kings 16:34. It says that a man called Hiel built Jericho and he laid in the foundations Abiram his firstborn, and set up the gates in his youngest son, Segub. That means that when he was building the city he killed two of his children and put their bodies in the foundations and under the gate-posts. By doing that Hiel thought that he was offering a sacrifice that would please God. We know that God would never want a sacrifice like that or worship like that and no one would ever think so if he really listened to God and paid heed to God. There is only one real worship of God. Worshipping him does not mean going to Church on Sunday and then doing pretty much what we like through the week. It was said of a great Greek that he lived all his life as if he were in a temple of the gods; and another great Greek said, "To be good is the only true worship of God." Real worship means living every moment of life remembering that we are in the presence of God and trying to make everything we do so good that it is fit to offer to him and so fine that it is fit for him to see.

The Fall of a Kingdom

In 721 B.C. the Northern Kingdom was destroyed forever. Disaster came to it because the people forgot God's benefits; disobeyed God's commands; disregarded God's messengers; and so came to worship God altogether in the wrong way. If we would live well we must never forget the gifts God has given to us; we must always do what he wants us to do; we must never disregard the warnings life brings to us; and we must worship him by living a lovely life every day.

QUESTIONS FOR DISCUSSION

1. Think of some of the things which as citizens and persons we owe to God.

2. Who are God's messengers to us today?

3. Are there any ways in which people today try to worship God in the wrong way?

8. HEZEKIAH, THE GOOD KING WHOSE PRAYER GOD ANSWERED

Hezekiah, the good King

We have seen how the Northern Kingdom perished utterly and how its inhabitants were taken away to far-off Assyria.

Now we must turn our thoughts to the Southern Kingdom, the two tribes who still had their capital at Jerusalem. As in the case of the Northern Kingdom we cannot trace the history of the Southern Kingdom in detail. All we can do is to look first at one of its great kings and then at its captivity. The good king's name was Hezekiah and he reigned in Jerusalem from 725 B.C. until 696 B.C.

Hezekiah, the Reformer

In a double sense Hezekiah was a reformer. He was a religious reformer. 2 Kings 18:4 tells us how he cleared out all the false worship and the worship of idols all over the country. One special thing Hezekiah tried to do. We get an echo of it in 2 Kings 18:22. There the taunt of his enemies is that he took away the high places and the altars and ordered the people to worship and to sacrifice in Jerusalem and in Jerusalem alone. What happened was this. We know that in Jesus' time the only place where sacrifice could be made and offered was the Temple in Jerusalem. If a man wished to make his sacrifice and his offering to God it was there that he had to come. But in Hezekiah's day there were altars in every village and priests in every village, and sacrifice could be made almost anywhere. We might think that to be a good thing and maybe in theory it was; but in practice it was a bad thing. Always remember this: when the children of Israel came into Palestine the land was not empty; the Canaanites were living there; and the children of Israel never totally cleared them out. Some of the original inhabitants were always there. Now the original inhabitants were Baal worshippers; and we have already seen how degraded Baal worship could be. What happened was that these local shrines were always liable to be infected with Baal worship; the things that the Baal worshippers did were always liable to creep in; and there was no control. It was to keep the worship of God clean and pure that it had all to be centralised in Jerusalem. Hezekiah was the first man to see how dangerous these local shrines and altars could be and how important it was to have everything in Jerusalem where it could be kept under control and clean and pure. Of course many people resented this. But Hezekiah was right and he was a brave man to shut down the local shrines and to make the Temple at Jerusalem the centre of the nation's worship. But Hezekiah was also a *social* reformer. In 2 Kings 20:20 we read how Hezekiah made a pool and a conduit and brought water into the city. One of the troubles of Jerusalem was that it never had a good water supply. Hezekiah was a great engineer and he dug a tunnel through the solid rock which can be seen to this day and brought to Jerusalem a water supply better than ever it had before.

Danger draws near

We have already seen how Samaria was captured by Shalmaneser and how Samaria fell. 2 Kings 18:9-12 very briefly retells that tragic story. Now this was a very real threat to Hezekiah. Remember how small a land Palestine was. Samaria was no more than 50 miles away from Jerusalem. The Assyrians were almost on Hezekiah's doorstep. Very soon Sennacherib, the next king of Assyria, turned his attention to the Southern Kingdom. This time Hezekiah was able to buy safety, but it cost him the gold and the silver in the Temple to buy it. He had to strip the Temple of its costly decorations to pay the tribute that Sennacherib demanded for leaving Jerusalem in peace (2 Kings 18:13-16). But it was a safety which was only a respite. Back came Sennacherib's commanders. In 2 Kings 18:17 we read of the Tartan, the Rabsaris and the Rabshakeh. None of these is a proper name; they are titles of military and state officials. For instance, the Tartan was the commander-in-chief of the Assyrian forces. They came and they hurled the most terrible threats at Hezekiah; they said that many another nation had tried to stand against Assyria and had perished; they said that all the nations had their gods and none of these gods had availed to stop the tide of Assyrian progress. So, they said, Hezekiah had better give in because his cause was hopeless (2 Kings 18:17-35). In his extremity Hezekiah asked the advice of Isaiah, the great prophet, and Isaiah told him not to be afraid; things might look black, but Jerusalem would yet be safe (2 Kings 19:1-7).

The same story is told in Isaiah, chapters 36 and 37. Still further troubles came to worry Hezekiah. The Assyrians sent him a threatening letter, and humanly speaking, it seemed that Hezekiah could not possibly have any hope against the Assyrian hordes; but Hezekiah took the letter into the Temple and spread it before God. He took his troubles to God (2 Kings 19:8-34). So the Assyrians set to to besiege the city and it seemed that there was no possible defence. And then one night there came a terrible blow to the Assyrian army. We are told that 185,000 of them perished in one night and Jerusalem was saved (2 Kings 19:35-37). There are some who think that Psalm 46 was written at this time as a great song of thanksgiving to God for this wonderful deliverance. Whether or not that is so, if we will read it we will see that it is peculiarly appropriate to a situation like this.

God's Hand in History

The story of the deliverance is written in 2 Kings 19:35. "The angel of the Lord went forth, and slew a hundred and eighty-five thousand in the camp of the Assyrians; and when men arose early in the morning, behold, these were all dead bodies." We may well ask what actually happened. It so happens that we have a variety of accounts of this terrible incident. We have this account in 2 Kings. We have the wonderful poem that Byron the poet made out of the incident.

The Assyrian came down like a wolf on the fold,
And his cohorts were gleaming in purple and gold;
And the sheen of their spears was like stars on the sea,
When the blue wave rolls nightly on deep Galilee.

Like the leaves of the forest when summer is green,
The host with their banners at sunset were seen;
Like the leaves of the forest when autumn hath blown,
The host on the morrow lay wither'd and strown.

For the Angel of Death spread his wings on the blast,
And breathed in the face of the foe as he passed:
And the eyes of the sleepers waxed deadly and chill,
And their hearts but once heaved and forever grew still.

And there lay the steed with his nostril all wide,
But through it there rolled not the breath of his pride;
And the foam of his gasping lay white on the turf,
And cold as the spray of the rock-beating surf.

And there lay the rider distorted and pale,
With the dew on his brow and the rust on his mail;
And the tents were all silent, the banners alone,
The lances unlifted, the trumpet unblown.

And the widows of Ashur are loud in their wail,
And the idols are broke in the temple of Baal;
And the might of the Gentile, unsmote by the sword,
Hath melted like snow in the glance of the Lord.

That is how the poet saw it. Now it so happens that there was a Greek historian, Herodotus, who was writing about a disaster that happened to Sennacherib within 50 years of the very event. He has this queer statement, that mice gnawed the string of the bows and the thongs of the shield of the Assyrian army and they were rendered helpless and had to retire and go home. What is the meaning? In Greek symbolism mice and rats stand for the terrible bubonic plague—and indeed they do carry it; and what most likely happened is that a terrible outbreak of bubonic plague smote Sennacherib's army and he had to go home. The question is—was the Hebrew historian right when he called it the smiting of the Angel of the Lord? He was undoubtedly right and there is a lesson for everyone to learn. It is often put this way. It is said that the Hebrews know nothing of *secondary causes*. If there is rain and thunder and lightning we say that certain atmospheric conditions caused the rain and the thunder and the lightning; we attribute it to atmospheric causes. The Hebrew would say, God sent the rain, God thundered, God spoke in the lightning. The Hebrew saw the hand of God in everything—and he was right. Just think how a Hebrew historian would have described the miracle of Dunkirk. During the embarkation there were mists, there was a calm and there were quite unusually high tides which made embarkation possible. The Hebrew would have written something like this: "The people went forth to battle against their enemies and the battle went sorely against them. So their enemies drove them to the sea beaches and they were in sore peril of their lives. So then the people prayed to God and God sent a cloud to hide them from their enemies; and God made of the waters a calm and made them to rise upon the shores of the sea; and so the ships came and God's hand delivered his people from their enemies." That would be precisely true. The Hebrew saw God's hand, God's angel in everything in all the world; and the Hebrew was right. It is God who sends the rain and the calm and the sun and the storm; it is God who rules the events of history and who sent disaster in Sennacherib's army and who delivered our own people in the day of trouble. It would be very much better if we saw things more like the Hebrew historian and said, "God did it." We are far too apt to leave God out of account. In the plague that smote the Assyrian army the Hebrew historian saw God's angel—he was right. God is always in control.

God's Deliverance

So Jerusalem was saved. Hezekiah's prayer was answered. It is true that the threat was not removed entirely. Isaiah warned Hezekiah that the day of disaster would surely come, but Hezekiah ended his days in peace (2 Kings 20:14-21).

The Man Who swept away Abuses

Let us now look at this man who "did what was right in the eyes of the Lord" (2 Kings 18:3) and after whom "there was none like him among all the kings of Judah after him, nor among those who were before him" (2 Kings 18:5). First of all, Hezekiah was *a man who began by waging war against abuses*. He saw that the local shrines were evil and he cleared them out. He saw that the city lacked for water and he brought water in. In this world there are two kinds of people. There are people who know quite well that there is something wrong and who do nothing about it. And there are people who, when they see that something is wrong, cannot rest until they have taken action to mend it. So many of us see what is wrong, but never do anything about it. Sometimes we just cannot be bothered; it is too much trouble. Sometimes we leave it to someone else; let someone else worry. Sometimes we are afraid to do anything; it would make us unpopular or we would get up against people who are influential or important. We have got to remember two things. First, to see that something is wrong and not to do anything about it is to be guilty of a sin. Every wrong thing should be a challenge to action. Second, no one has any right to criticise unless he is prepared to do something about the situation which he is criticising. It is easy to see and to talk; what God wants is action. Hezekiah brought action to a bad situation; that is why he was a great and a good king. We would not think much of a doctor who was able only to diagnose, who could tell you what was wrong, but who never thought of doing anything to make you better. We must not only be able to diagnose what is wrong in any situation; we must be ready and willing and eager and brave enough to do something about it.

The Man of Prayer

But second, Hezekiah was *a man of prayer*. When he was faced with a terrible situation he spread it before God (2 Kings 19:14). That is what all great men have done. Abraham Lincoln said, "I would be the greatest fool on earth if I did not realise that I could never satisfy the demands of this high office without the help of One who is greater and stronger than I am." In the 1914-18 war there was a military conference. The commander-in-chief, Field-Marshal Foch, was not there. Someone who knew him said, "I think I know where he can be found." He led them to a little ruined chapel and there was Foch praying before the altar. Field-Marshal Montgomery said, "Every night I pray that I may not be allowed to fail my men." The reason why we so often fail in life is that we try to do things ourselves. The reason why we so often collapse is that we try to do it all in our own strength. We do not need to. The hymn is right when it tells us to take everything to the Lord in prayer. If we knew of a man who had at his disposal the greatest forces and powers and who never used them we would say that he was a very foolish man. That is exactly what we do if we never pray. Every morning we should ask God's help for the day. It may be that we have time only to pray the prayer that old Sir Jacob Astley prayed before battle, "Thou knowest how busy I will be today; if I forget Thee, do not Thou forget me." If we are up against it, with some specially hard things to do, some specially difficult task to face, some specially strong temptation to conquer we should always speak to God about it. On 16th November 1941, in the blackest days of the war, Sir Winston Churchill told Field-Marshal Lord Alanbrooke that he was to succeed Sir John Dill as Chief of the Imperial General Staff. The Field-Marshal wrote in his Diary:

"I am not an exceptionally religious person but I am not ashamed to confess that as soon as he was out of the room, my first impulse was to kneel down and pray to God for guidance and support in the task I had undertaken. As I look back at the years that followed I can now see clearly how well this prayer was answered."

There is a story about a man who found it hard to pray. A saintly friend said to him, "Just sit down and put a chair opposite you and imagine that God is in that chair and just talk to him." All his life he did it. And when he died they found him lying in bed with an empty chair drawn up at the side of the bed. He had been talking to God. Like Hezekiah we will find strength to do the impossible if we always remember to pray to God.

The Man God delivered

Lastly, Hezekiah was the man who set out to right abuses and the man who prayed *and therefore God helped him*. There are two things about God we must remember. First, God only helps those who help themselves. God must never be looked upon as a kind of easy way out. It is only when we have done our best that God comes in. Second, there is a strange courtesy about God. God does not ordinarily—although he sometimes does—force himself upon us. He waits for us to ask him. But if we do our best and then ask his help he never fails us.

The Good King

Hezekiah was the king who set out to put to rights the abuses in his kingdom. He was the man who took everything to God. He was the man whom God delivered. Hezekiah was the good king because he did the right thing and asked God to help him.

QUESTIONS FOR DISCUSSION

1. What abuses still need reformation in this country?

2. It has been said that first we must pray and that then we must work our hardest to make our prayers come true. What ought we to pray for and to work for?

3. Does God always deliver the good man in this life? What can we say when we see goodness suffering and defeated?

9. THE DESOLATION OF JERUSALEM

The Beginning of Disaster

We have already seen how Palestine lay in the most dangerous position of the ancient world. It lay exactly between Egypt and the great empires of the east. Palestine is the only land bridge between Africa and Asia and therefore if these great empires were ever to close in battle with each other there was no other way for them to march than through Palestine. It was precisely that fact that brought Palestine to disaster and brought final ruin to the Southern Kingdom and to Jerusalem. The power to the south was Egypt; by this time the power to the north and the east was Babylon, for the Babylonian Empire had now succeeded the Assyrian. The Southern Kingdom in all its littleness and its comparative helplessness was like a nut between the two arms of a mighty nut-cracker. It seemed impossible that it could avoid being crushed out of existence.

So for the Southern Kingdom from 608 B.C. until 586 B.C. there came 22 terrible years when the end was rushing on.

The good King Dies

The beginning of the end came in 608 B.C. In that year Pharaoh Neco (all Egyptian kings were called Pharaoh) decided to invade the kingdom of Babylon. To get there, as we have seen, he had to pass through Palestine. At that time the king of the Southern Kingdom was Josiah. He was the finest of all the kings. It was in his time that the Book of Deuteronomy had been discovered in the Temple and in obedience to the laws of that great book he had reformed his kingdom. He was a man of justice and of kindness, a king intimately known to his subjects, always accessible to them, a man greatly beloved. He could easily have sought safety. But he went out to seek to stop Pharaoh Neco. There was a battle at Megiddo and the end was tragedy, for, as the Book of Kings vividly says, Pharaoh Neco "slew him at Megiddo when he saw him" (2 Kings 23:29, 30; cp. 2 Chron. 35:20-24). It seems that in the very first moment of the battle Josiah, the good king, fell mortally wounded; and then chaos descended upon the country.

The foolish King

The people chose Jehoahaz (2 Kings 23:30), one of Josiah's sons, to be king; but he reigned for only three months. Then the Egyptians banished him, imposed a crushing tribute on the land, and installed his brother on the throne (2 Kings 23:33, 34). It was clear that the Southern Kingdom was no longer its own master; it was at the mercy of Egypt. At this time one of the greatest figures in the Southern Kingdom was the prophet Jeremiah; and Jeremiah wrote a dirge for Jehoahaz as he went away to a captivity from which he was never to return.

"Weep not for him who is dead,
    nor bemoan him;
  but weep bitterly for him who goes away,
    for he shall return no more
    to see his native land.

For thus says the Lord concerning Shallum (Shallum is another name for Jehoahaz) the son of Josiah, king of Judah, who reigned instead of Josiah his father, and who went away from this place: 'He shall return here no more, but in the place where they have carried him captive, there shall he die, and he shall never see this land again'" (Jer. 22:10-12).

After a brief three months' reign the young prince was banished forever and he was only twenty-three (2 Kings 23:31). The name of the new king whom the Egyptians set on the throne was Jehoiakim (2 Kings 23:34).

This Jehoiakim acted in a way that was little short of mad. Remember that the land was under threat. It was, or should have been, clear for all to see that the nation stood on the very edge of the abyss. 2 Kings does not tell us very much about Jehoiakim, but Jeremiah does. For one thing he taxed the people till he bled them white (2 Kings 23:35). The people might have understood that there was no other way in which Egypt could be appeased. But at a time like this the insane Jehoiakim developed a passion for building; and in order to gratify it he employed his people and gave them no wages and made them slaves. Justice was forgotten. Jeremiah rebuked him and reminded him of the fine example of his father, Josiah; but still even in the hour of desperate peril Jehoiakim went upon his foolish way (Jer. 22:13-19).

The Prophet who faced the Truth

Throughout all this time Jeremiah was facing the truth and speaking for God. He was the one man in the kingdom who cared to look facts in the face. There were false prophets who said, "You shall have peace" (Jer. 23:17), but Jeremiah knew that the end was on the way and that nothing could stop it. By this time Egypt as a great power had faded out and the power was Babylon. Nebuchadnezzar of Babylon had arrived at the gates of Jerusalem and Jehoiakim had become his vassal. But the statesmen of the Southern Kingdom wriggled this way and that and sought this escape and that. Only Jeremiah saw and told them plainly that there was no escape (Jer. 25:9-11 and many other passages). So in Jerusalem there was a mad situation. Jehoiakim went on with his forced levies and his building which made people slaves which was as good as fiddling while Rome was burning; the statesmen tried this and that plan to avoid the inevitable end; the people bitterly resented the taxation and the slavery imposed on them; and only one man, Jeremiah, faced the truth. Jehoiakim's utter folly is vividly shown in one incident. Jeremiah wished to send him a message of warning. He was not able to take it himself so he had it written by Baruch the scribe and sent to Jehoiakim. And Jehoiakim was actually guilty of the incredible folly of cutting the message up and burning it in the fire (Jer. 16:1-23). There can be nothing but disaster for a man who treats God's messages like that.

The Tragic King

In the end Jehoiakim died; but in his reign he had only succeeded by his almost incredible folly in making a bad situation worse than it was. A situation which had been serious had now become incurable. He was succeeded by Jehoiachin. He was only a lad of eighteen years of age. Hardly had he mounted the throne than Nebuchadnezzar's armies were at the gates of Jerusalem. He had the sense to see that there was nothing left for it but surrender; and surrender he did. And so, in 596 B.C., the first step of the final end came; for the Babylonian armies entered the city, despoiled the temple; carried off into the exile the best of the people and all the craftsmen; and left behind a weakened, a poverty-stricken and an almost desolate city. The Southern Kingdom was launched on the way to destruction (2 Kings 24:10-16).

The Destruction of Jerusalem

Although Nebuchadnezzar had conquered Jerusalem he was kindly enough to leave the kingdom a semblance of independence. He put on the throne a man called Zedekiah. Now Jeremiah was still there, still bluntly speaking the truth and still bluntly speaking for God. He insisted that nothing but harm could come of resistance and there was nothing left for the people to do but to submit (Jer. 21:3-10 and many other passages). But Zedekiah was ill-advised. He went on intriguing and plotting, and in the end the armies of Nebuchadnezzar descended upon Jerusalem. After a siege the city was starved into subjection. Zedekiah himself attempted escape; but he was captured; his sons were killed before him and then his eyes were put out (2 Kings 25:1-7). This time the Babylonians were thorough. They burned the city and destroyed the Temple and carried away the rest of the people to Babylon; and Jerusalem became an empty and a terrible desolation. Like the Northern Kingdom now the Southern Kingdom, too, was wiped out, and, apparently the end had come. In 586 B.C. the Southern Kingdom ceased to exist.

The Refusal to face the Facts

Now there were certain quite discernible reasons why this disaster took place; and we do well to study them, for the foolishness of these last terrible mad days was the kind of foolishness that we can very easily repeat in our own lives and which could also make shipwreck of them. For one thing, all through those days *people refused to face the facts*. It was quite clear that they could never resist Babylon, that there was nothing to do but to accept the situation, but they refused to see it. The false prophets went on saying that everything would be all right; Jehoiakim went on with his grandiose building schemes; Zedekiah went on with his plotting; Jeremiah alone faced the facts. If we are ever going to do anything with life we must begin by facing the facts. Suppose a man was ill; suppose he was obviously ill; suppose his doctor told him he was ill and that if he did not accept treatment he would die; then suppose that man just refused to face the facts and went on living just as he liked; and then suppose he died; you would quite justly say that he had no one to blame but himself. It is never any good shutting our eyes to the facts. We must be open-eyed to the facts about ourselves. The most valuable knowledge that a man can have is knowledge of himself. We must be well aware of our own weaknesses. It is a very valuable thing to know just what we can do and just what we cannot do. If we have some bad habit, for instance, it is easy to shut our eyes to it. We have got to face facts and root it out. If some one tells us that if we go on as we are doing it will cause no end of trouble, it is easy to disregard that good advice; but it is the height of foolishness not to face the facts. It is easy and natural to push some unpleasant truth or fact into the background; but it is folly. We must always be honest enough and brave enough to face the facts.

Listening to the wrong People

For another thing all through those days *people listened to the wrong people*. They listened to the false prophets who told them that everything would be all right; and they refused to listen to Jeremiah who told them the unpleasant and unwelcome truth. Always in life we will get people who want us to do the wrong things. Sometimes they can make it very attractive. They tell us that there is no harm in such and such a thing; that everybody does it; that it will be quite all right if we do it. And there are always people who love us and who wish to keep us in the right way; and often the things they tell us to do are hard and difficult things. They sometimes have to stop us doing what we want to do and make us do things that we do not want to do. A very wise old Greek used to say, "Listen to what your enemies say about you because they will see your faults before you do." It is sometimes very hard to listen to those who criticise us, but it is to our good. This means that we must be very careful whom we choose as our friends. Charles Kingsley was a great friend of a saintly man called F. D. Maurice. Kingsley was once asked how he succeeded in living so fine a life. He answered, "I had a friend." When Robert Burns was a young man he was sent to Irvine to learn flax-dressing. There he met a man who was both foolish and wicked. Burns said of him afterwards, "His friendship did me a mischief." Kingsley's friend made him; Burns' friend marred him. We must choose our friends wisely and well; and we must choose the best of all friends—Jesus Himself.

Politics instead of God

For still one other thing, *the people of the Southern Kingdom tried to find safety in politics rather than in God.* The people of the Southern Kingdom tried to mend things by political alliances and the like. Jeremiah wanted them to mend things by cleaning up their own lives and by obeying God, and Jeremiah was right. We are very like that today. We say, Give a man a better house, a better job, better wages, better working conditions, social security, and you will change the country. Now all these are good things and things that the Church must support. But there is no good giving a man a better house or a better job or a better wage, and leaving him the same man. It is not enough to change things and conditions; the only thing that is enough is to change people, and only God can do that. It is only Jesus who can make people less selfish, more forgiving, less bitter, kinder to each other. The only person who can really make a better world is God and it is only when men give their hearts to Him that the better world will come. It is only when all men love Jesus that they will love each other. We can bring that day nearer by taking Jesus as *our* Master and *our* Lord.

The End of a Kingdom

The Southern Kingdom fell because men refused to face the facts; because they listened to the wrong people; because they put their trust in politics instead of God. These are mistakes that we must never make.

QUESTIONS FOR DISCUSSION

1. Are there any things in our national life at present which could cause the ruin of the nation?

2. How far ought the Church to take part in politics?

3. Do Church members take a big enough part in the leadership of the community and of the state?

10. IN EXILE

A People's Exile

We have seen how first the Northern Kingdom in 721 B.C. and then the Southern Kingdom in 586 B.C. were both destroyed; and we have seen how the great majority of the inhabitants of both kingdoms were carried away into exile. Now we must remember one thing about this exile. It was not like the exile of one man exiled, say, to Siberia. It was the exile of a people. The kings and the princes, the rulers and the statesmen, the craftsmen and the tradesmen and the ordinary people were all taken away together (2 Kings 24:10-16). It was a whole people which was taken away. It was therefore possible for them to take up life again as a people in a foreign land. True, they were no longer independent. Strangers were their masters, but all the same they could still live as a community in the land to which they had been taken. But there is another thing and a most important thing that we must remember. It was not like the exile of a man to some barren and deserted and lonely place as, say, when Napoleon was exiled to the little island of Elba. The odd and unusual thing about the exile of the Jews was that it was as if you had taken a group of country people and set them down quite suddenly in the middle of London or New York. Palestine was a very little land; Jerusalem was not really a very big city. But Babylon was one of the greatest cities in the world. There the Jews would see buildings the like of which they had never seen before. They would see great temples beside which the Temple in Jerusalem would appear small and insignificant; they would see a wealth and a trade and a commerce of a richness that they had never dreamed of. So far from being taken into some lonely desert place they were taken amongst the greatest cities, in the greatest empire, in the richest civilisation in the world.

A People's Danger

Just because of that the people of Israel ran a very grave danger. It would have been the easiest thing in the world for them to lose their identity. They could easily have forgotten their native customs, forgotten their own religion, even forgotten their own language. They could easily have been swallowed up in this great mass until they stopped being Jews altogether and became Babylonians. It is very easy for a person to lose his own characteristics and to become like the people amongst whom he lives. We have known, for instance, Scots people who went to England to live and to work and in a few years they learned to speak in such a way that you would never have known that they were Scots; and they learned to live in such a way that you would never have known that they had been brought up in a Scottish tradition. It would have been the easiest thing in the world for the Jews to lose themselves among the people in whose midst they had been forced to dwell.

The People who remained themselves

That is indeed what did happen to the ten tribes who were taken away captive from Samaria in 721 B.C. They were taken away to Assyria; in time they ceased to be Israelites and became like the Assyrians; in time they were completely lost among the Assyrians; they did in fact vanish from history as a people; and to this day men call them the lost ten tribes. But it was the very opposite with the people who were taken away to Babylon from the Southern Kingdom and from Jerusalem in 586 B.C. Babylon might be a great land and a rich land and a land in which it would have been easy to lose themselves but they stubbornly refused to be anything else but Jews. They might be surrounded by splendid temples, far greater than their own Temple, with a worship far more magnificent than their worship; but they stubbornly refused to forget God. "If I forget you, O Jerusalem," they sang, "let my right hand wither! Let my tongue cleave to the roof of my mouth, if I do not remember you, if I do not set Jerusalem above my highest joy" (Ps. 137:5, 6). They would not and they could not ever forget that they were Jews. That is a wonderful thing. Jesus was a Jew; and if the Jews of the Southern Kingdom had forgotten their native land and their God as the Jews of the Northern Kingdom did, the Jews would have vanished from history and God could not have raised up his Son amidst the Jews at all.

Faith in a Destiny

There were certain things which enabled the Jews to maintain their identity in Babylon when they might so easily have lost it. For one thing, *they were conscious of being different from other people*. And the difference, as they saw it, lay in this—they were quite sure that, even though the present situation looked like disaster, God still had a task that he meant them to do. There are three ways of feeling different from other people; there is a right way and a wrong way. It is possible to feel *superior* to other people. It is possible to look down on other people. Jesus once told a story about a Pharisee who stood in the Temple and who thanked God that he was not as other men are (Luke 18:11, 12). There is a record of a Jewish Pharisee who said, "If there are only two righteous people in the world, I and my son are these two. If there is only one righteous man in the world, I am that man." That sense of being different is quite wrong. Anything that makes us think ourselves better than other people is not a good thing. But again, it is possible to feel different from others in the sense that we may feel that there is laid upon us *a greater responsibility* than there is on other people. We may feel that there are some things which other people may be able to do, but we cannot do them. The finest soldiers in the world are the Brigade of Guards. When our troops were waiting to be taken off the beaches at Dunkirk and when most people, very naturally, had little thought beyond somehow gaining safety, the Guards actually held a kit inspection and appeared freshly shaved. When they did get off the boats in England they marched off with the same precision as if they were changing the Guard in London. It might be all right for some people to lower their standards a bit when things were desperate and when they were tired, but the Guards could not do things like that. They were different. It should be so with us. That is a good way to be different for it means that we are different because we have a sense of responsibility for living up to the standards of our faith. But still again, we may have a feeling of being different because God has given us *a special task* to do. That was the way in which the Jews in Babylon felt different. They might at the moment be captives and strangers and exiles in a foreign land, but for all that, they were still sure that God had some special task for their nation to do in the world. Now God has a special task for everyone to do. Someone has finely said that everyone of us is an idea of God. Now suppose a young man is chosen to play football or cricket or to run for his country. That means he knows that he has a special job to do. He will, therefore, deny himself many things that other people allow themselves; he will accept a discipline that many other people think quite unnecessary and he will do this because of his sense of the importance of the task that has been given him to do. That makes him feel different. The Jews succeeded in remaining different and in keeping their faith intact because they were sure God had a task for them to do. We, too, must feel that God has a special plan and a special task for us. Maybe we do not know yet what it is, but it is there and we must keep ourselves clean and fine as we wait for it. Sometimes it will be difficult to be different. Once Joan of Arc wanted to set out on an exploit that everyone else said was too difficult. She answered, "I do not think it can be very difficult if God is on your side and you are willing to put your life in his hand." When we put our lives into God's hand even the hard things become possible.

A Day and a Book

Still further, the Jews in Babylon succeeded in maintaining their identity because they had two things which could not be taken away from them—*they had their Day and their Book*. There were many things that they could not do in Babylon. For instance, they could no longer offer sacrifice in the Temple courts. But no one could take the Sabbath day away from them and no one could take from them God's Book and God's Law. At the time, of course, away back in 586 B.C., much of the Old Testament had still to be written and the New Testament was not in existence at all; but even then the Jews had the Law and no one could take the Law from them. We, too, have these two things. We have Sunday, the Lord's Day. If we use that day as we ought it will help us to be different from others. The great use of Sunday is just this: on the ordinary days of the week we are so busy at work that we have no time really to sit down and think about God. But on the Sunday all these things are laid aside. We go to Church; and in Church we remember God. It is bound to make us different if every Sunday we think about God and remember what he has done for us and what he wants us to do. Sunday is the day to think of God. We have the Book and we have an even more valuable Book than the Jews had for we have the whole Old Testament and the whole New Testament too. Sometimes when you are on a journey either hiking or cycling or motoring and when you are not quite sure what road to take, someone says, "Let's get out the map and have a look at it." Sometimes when you are trying to make or to repair something and you are not quite sure what to do next, someone says, "Let's get out the book of instructions; it will tell us what to do." In God's Book we have a map for life and instruction for life. The Jews in Babylon succeeded in keeping their faith even amongst a heathen people because they had their Day and their Book. We still have these things and if we use them wisely and well it will help us to live as Christians should live.

Coming together

One other thing the Jews had. Even in Babylon there was one thing that could not be taken away from them. They had their meeting together on the Sabbath to read the Book, to pray to God and to listen to God's word. They were not left to try to be different all alone. They were doing this job and facing this task together and that made all the difference. That is one of the things where we are very fortunate. We have got the Church. We are not trying to live Christian lives all alone; we are one of a group, of a company, of a fellowship who are doing things together. We ought never to think that we can get on all right in the Christian life alone. We should always come together with others who are aiming at the same things as those at which we are aiming.

Keeping the Faith in Babylon

Even in Babylon, when it would have been so easy to lose their identity and to be lost in the great nation amongst whom they dwelt, the Jews kept their identity and kept their faith. They did so because they had a sense of being different. We should never feel different in the sense of feeling superior to others; but we should feel that we have a responsibility to live a different and a finer life than those who have not Jesus for their master; and we should feel a responsibility to be different because we know that we have a task from God which some day we must do. They did so because they had and they used God's Day and God's Book. They did so because they met and worshipped God together. We have the same duty of keeping ourselves different from the world—and we have an even greater help than all these things. We have Jesus with us all the way.

QUESTIONS FOR DISCUSSION

1. What is the difference between feeling different from others and feeling superior to others?

2. What tasks does God give to Christians today?

3. What would you say to someone who argued that you can be a Christian without going to Church?

11. THE EXILES RETURN

The Jews come back to Jerusalem

We have now seen how both the Northern and the Southern Kingdoms were wiped out and how their inhabitants were carried away respectively to Assyria and to Babylon. Further, we have seen how the people of the Northern Kingdom lost their identity in the foreign land to which they were taken and how they vanished from history; and we have seen how, on the other hand, the people of the Southern Kingdom stubbornly refused to forget that they were Jews and clung tenaciously to their faith in God and to their own religion. There is nothing quite so strong as the pull of home upon men's hearts and the longing for their own native land. Robert Louis Stevenson was never a strong man; he had to leave Scotland and go away and live in the South Sea Islands; but even in the warmth and the richness of the South Seas he never forgot the bare, bleak hills and moors of his own land. And in that memory he wrote:

Be it granted to me to behold you again in dying
    Hills of home! and to hear again the call;
Hear about the graves of the martyrs the peewees crying,
    And hear no more at all.

There is a famous poem written by an unknown exiled Scot called the Canadian Boat Song. Its first verse is:

From the lone shieling and the misty island
    Mountains divide us and a waste of seas;
But still our hearts are true, our hearts are highland
    And we in dreams behold the Hebrides.

That is just how the Jews felt. Away in far-off, wealthy Babylon they never forgot their own land.

It was, as we saw, in 586 B.C. that they were carried away from Jerusalem to Babylon. Almost 50 years later there came to some of them the opportunity to return. It was the Babylonians who had carried them away. But a new power arose in the East, the power of the Persians, and the Persians conquered Babylon. Now the Persians were a peculiarly fine people. Every Persian boy was taught to do two things: to ride straight and to tell the truth. And the Persians had one special characteristic— they respected the gods of every people. Wherever they went and wherever they conquered they gave orders that the shrines of their captive peoples' religions should be carefully looked after. It was in 539 B.C. that Cyrus conquered Babylon and in the next year he gave orders for certain of the Jews to return home to rebuild the Temple of their God (Ezra 1).

The First Return

So the Jews did return home, but not very many of them went. They did rebuild the Temple, but the country was in a sorry state. There was continual opposition from the people who had been left behind and who had remained behind in Palestine; and worse—the people were dull and dispirited; and they drifted away from God. It was during this time that the little Book of Malachi was written. And Malachi had some hard things to say of them. When they brought animals that were to be sacrificed they were often maimed and imperfect and blemished. Malachi asked them, "If you were to bring animals like that to the governor of the country, what would he say and how would he like it? And yet you bring them to God" (Mal. 1:6-10). The whole business of worshipping God was a weariness to them (Mal. 1:13). There was no difference between being good and bad. God did not care (Mal. 2:17; 3:13-15). In the modern phrase, these first returned exiles just could not care less. Jerusalem was a dull and dead and unhappy place.

Nehemiah hears the News

Almost a century passed by in that unhappy way and then there arose a man who not only rebuilt Jerusalem, but who also rebuilt the faith of his people. His name was Nehemiah. He was a Jew, but in Babylon he had risen to the highest rank to which any man could rise. He was the cup-bearer of Artaxerxes the king (Neh. 2:1). News filtered through to Babylon of the sorry state of things in Jerusalem and Nehemiah's heart was pierced with sorrow (Neh. 1:1-3). His sorrow was such that it showed upon his face. The king asked him what ailed him and Nehemiah told him and asked the king to allow him to go back to Jerusalem to try to mend things there. And the king graciously not only gave him permission to go, but gave him every possible assistance and help (Neh. 2:1-8). Nehemiah was a man of initiative and of drive. He soon got the work going. But he met with constant opposition. The people who had been left in the country did not want to see Jerusalem rebuilt. Sanballat and his friends who now lived in Samaria saw well enough that if Jerusalem rose from its ruins their power and position would no longer be pre-eminent. The last thing they wanted was to see Jerusalem rise from the ruins (Neh. 2:9, 10). They tried mockery; they said that a fox could knock down the wall that Nehemiah's men were building (Neh. 4:1-6); but Nehemiah went right on. They tried threats so that even Nehemiah's friends grew afraid for his safety and advised him to hide in the Temple. But Nehemiah said, "A man like me does not run away," and went right on (Neh. 6:1-14). They even tried slander, saying that Nehemiah's idea in rebuilding the wall was to stage a rebellion against the Persians (Neh. 6:6); but the mud would not stick and still Nehemiah went on. Nehemiah set his men building with a tool in one hand and a weapon in the other (Neh. 4:13-18). He was ready for any emergency. Nehemiah had trouble in his own community. The people were very poor; the weather had been bad and the crops had failed; taxes had to be paid and the work of building the wall was done without payment at all. The result was that the poor had borrowed from the wealthy and could not now pay their debts; and the wealthy were cruelly about to sell the poor people into slavery. Nehemiah was angry. He saw that a desperate situation demanded desperate measures and he called a meeting of the people and made an arrangement that all debts were cancelled and all old scores were wiped out (Neh. 5:1-13). Nehemiah must have been a man of tremendous force of character to get a regulation like that passed by the people. So, in the end, in fifty-two days of almost frantic activity, the wall was built and Nehemiah had made of his shattered countrymen a nation once again (Neh. 6:15, 16). There is no more important figure in the story of the King and the Kingdom than Nehemiah for he can in truth be called the second founder of the nation.

The Man who was dependable

Now let us look at some of the characteristics of this man Nehemiah. First of all, Nehemiah was *the dependable man*. As we have seen he was the king's cup-bearer. In the East in the old days the king's life was always under threat. There were always those who wished to usurp the throne; and the king was never safe from assassination. Poison was one of the favourite ways of murdering a king; therefore the king's cup-bearer was a man who literally had the king's life in his hands. He was a man on whom the king had to be able to rely utterly and absolutely. Nehemiah was like that. Artaxerxes entrusted his life into Nehemiah's hands. Alexander the Great had a doctor whom he trusted like that. Once Alexander was ill and the doctor was prescribing for him. Every day the doctor brought Alexander a draught of medicine to drink. One day Alexander received a slanderous letter that the doctor was out to poison him. The doctor came with the draught of medicine. Alexander first drank the medicine and then handed the doctor the letter to read. He so showed the doctor how much he trusted him. That is the way in which Artaxerxes trusted Nehemiah. In this world we will never get anywhere unless we are dependable. It is not brilliant people the world wants nearly so much as people on whom they can rely absolutely. No one has any use for the kind of person who promises to do something and then does not do it. No one has any use for the person who leaves things half done. No one has any use for the person who lets us down, or who is one thing to our face and another behind our back. It does not matter how clever a person is, if he is not dependable and reliable he will never be a worthwhile man.

The Man who got things done

Further, Nehemiah was *the man who got things done*. It might have daunted anyone to arrive in Jerusalem from Babylon and to find the city a heap of ruins; but Nehemiah was the man who was able to get things done. He got things done for two reasons. First, he was clearly a man who refused to admit that anything was impossible. It would have been the easiest thing in the world to look at the mass of ruins which was Jerusalem and to say that it was quite impossible to do anything about it. *Impossible* is a word that we should do our best to erase from our mind and from our vocabulary. One of the most famous engineering firms in America is called AiResearch. It was built up by a man called Clifford Garrett and it manufactures the extremely delicate instruments needed for flying at the amazing speeds and heights which are now necessary. Sometimes instruments had to be made to such delicate limits that other firms declared that it could not be done. Garrett hired a number of young men who had just finished their degrees and training in the technical schools and colleges. He said, "They did not know what was impossible, so they went ahead and did what we told them to do." A famous scientist once said, "The difference between what is difficult and what is impossible is that what is impossible takes a little longer to do." Nehemiah did not talk about things being impossible. He just set to and did them. Second, Nehemiah knew *how* to get things done, and how to turn the impossible into a fact. He had a principle by which he set his people rebuilding the wall—everyone rebuilt the little bit over against his own house (Neh. 3:28). Nehemiah knew well that if everyone got down to his own little bit the job would soon be done. Suppose there is a heavy fall of snow; the way to clear the pavements is for every shopkeeper and for every householder to clear the bit at his own door and very soon the whole pavement is clear. The only way to get things done is for every one of us to do his own bit. It is only when every person in the team is pulling his weight that the team really plays well. A Chinese once prayed this prayer, "Lord, revive Thy Church, *beginning with me.*" Nehemiah knew that the way to get things done was to make everyone do his bit. Things will really start to happen when each one of us puts everything he has got into every task he has got to do.

The brave Man

One other quality Nehemiah had — *Nehemiah was a man of courage*. When his enemies threatened his life some of his friends advised him to seek refuge in the Temple. In those days temples had what was called the right of asylum. If a hunted man in danger of his life could reach a temple and get into it, he was held to be safe and no one could hurt him. But when that suggestion was made to Nehemiah his answer was, "Should such a man as I flee?" (Neh. 6:10, 11). Nehemiah thought far too much of himself to run away. We may not think that we matter very much personally and as individuals. But besides being individuals we are members of the Church of Jesus Christ.

We will often be tempted to do mean or cowardly things, or to take up some course of action which is not quite true and not quite honest. When that happens we have got to say to ourselves, "One of Jesus' men cannot act like that."

The Man who rebuilt the Nation

Nehemiah rebuilt the walls of Jerusalem and he did an even bigger thing than that—he rebuilt his own people and his own nation. He succeeded because he was a man upon whom all could depend; he was a man who got things done because he did not know the meaning of the word impossible, and because he saw that team-work is the secret of success. He was a man who was brave because he knew that a man like him could never stoop to any cowardly way.

QUESTIONS FOR DISCUSSION

1. What kind of things do we fail to attempt, because we say that they are impossible?

2. What are the qualities of real patriotism?

3. What would you say to the criticism that in Persia Nehemiah was serving his country's conquerors?

12. FAITHFUL UNTO DEATH

Between the Testaments

We have seen how the Jews came back to Jerusalem and how they rebuilt their shattered city under the leadership of the gallant Nehemiah, and now we have to come to a part of history which is not related in the Old Testament but which is none the less of primary importance in the history of the King and the Kingdom. Although the story of this period which we are now to study does not find a place in the pages of the Old Testament it is told in one of those books which were written between the Testaments. It is told in the Books of the Maccabees which are what are called Apocryphal books. The Apocrypha, as they are called, literally mean the secret or the hidden books; and they got their name because the Church approved them for private and for home reading, but not for reading at the public worship of God as other books of the Bible are read. That is the meaning of the name, although it is true that they are still printed in many Bibles and some of them at least are read at public worship in the Church of England. Very many great things happened between the times of the Old and the New Testament and it is at some of the greatest and the most glorious that we must now look.

The Jewish State and the World Empires

One thing we must begin by noting—when the Jews came back from Babylon and settled down again in Jerusalem they became in the most definite and deliberate way the people of the Law. By a very deliberate act of choice they took God's Law upon them. In Neh. 8:1-8 we read how Ezra the scribe assembled the people, how he read the book of God's Law to them and how the people pledged themselves forever to obey it and forever to be a people of God's Law. They knew that they were so small a nation that they could not at that moment hope to be great in the political sense of the term and so they decided that they would devote all their strength and will and mind and heart to the obeying of God's Law. For about a hundred years things went on without any great interruptions. Then, in 366 B.C., there burst upon the world the greatest conqueror the world has ever seen. His name was Alexander the Great. He reigned for only twelve years; he died when he was only thirty-six; and before he died one day he was found in tears and when he was asked why, he answered, "Because there are no more worlds left to conquer." Starting from Macedonia in Greece, he conquered the whole world as far away as India. We may see something of the world greatness of Alexander when we remember that the romantic story of his conquests soon after his death existed in no fewer than twenty-four different languages. Palestine, like all the rest of the world, became part of Alexander's empire; but for the Jews it made little difference and life went on in the same way. Alexander died in 323 B.C. and then his empire disintegrated. It was the force of his personality that had held it together and when he died it became a seething cauldron of warring leaders and generals each trying to carve out a kingdom for himself. With only two of these are we concerned. Ptolemy, one of Alexander's generals, entrenched himself in Egypt; and Seleucus, another of his generals, set up his kingdom first in Babylon and later in Antioch, in Syria. Now these two kingdoms were forever at each other's throats; and Palestine was in the same old perilous position. There she stood, the little, almost helpless, kingdom, the bone of contention between the Ptolemaic and the Seleucid Empires, as they are called. Right down until 198 B.C. the Jews were part of the Empire of Egypt and of the Ptolemies, and in those days the Jews had nothing to complain of; they were well treated and they were allowed to worship in their own way and to keep their own law. It is true than often their country was a battle-ground, but they were not persecuted for their faith. Then, in 198 B.C., they fell into the power of the Syrian kings, the Seleucids, and their troubles began.

Antiochus Epiphanes

In 175 B.C. there came to the Syrian throne a king called Antiochus Epiphanes. His very name shows what kind of man he was. *Epiphanes* is short for *Theos Epiphanes*, which means *God Manifest*. This man claimed to be a god himself come down to earth. Now this man had one love and one hatred. He loved all things Greek, Greek language, Greek dress, Greek culture and, above all, Greek religion; and he believed it to be his mission in life to spread Greek religion and worship of the Greek gods all through his realms. He hated above all things the Jewish religion and swore he would exterminate it. He was utterly and fanatically and even madly determined to wipe out the very memory of the Jewish faith. He found renegade Jews who were very willing to help him. He found Jews, even in Jerusalem, were prepared to wear Greek dress, to speak the Greek language, to adopt Greek customs and to worship the Greek gods. But he found others who would not. So, in 168 B.C., he attacked Jerusalem. History has seldom or never seen such a cold-blooded attempt to wipe out a nation's faith. Eighty thousand men, women and children were killed and as many more sold into captivity as slaves. In the very Temple itself he set up an image of Olympian Zeus, the greatest of the Greek gods, and ordered that sacrifice should be made to it. In the Temple court he deliberately sacrificed swine, and swine to the Jews are unclean animals, and he defiled the Temple with their blood. He turned the chambers and rooms in the courts of the Temple into brothels. With a kind of terrible deliberation he desecrated the Temple. He made the possession of a copy of the Law a crime punishable by death. A parent who circumcised his child was promptly executed. His soldiers and inspectors were sent from house to house like inquisitors looking for copies of the Law so that every copy in the country might be destroyed. Never in history was such a deliberate attempt made to wipe out a faith.

The Heroes of the Faith

There are two of the most famous stories in Jewish history which come from this terrible killing time. The first is of an aged priest, called Eleazar. Antiochus's men tried to compel the old man to eat swine's flesh, which for a Jew is unclean. The old man answered, "No, not if you pluck out my eyes and consume my bowels in the fire" (4 Mac. 5:28). They bound him and scourged him until "his flesh was torn off by the whips and he streamed down with blood and his flanks were laid open by wounds". They deliberately kicked him as he lay prostrate in agony on the ground. The very soldiers themselves were moved with compassion and one suggested that he should bring ordinary meat and that Eleazar should pretend that it was swine's flesh and should eat it and so escape. The old man refused the deception and in the end they burned him to death (4 Mac. 6). Nothing would break the iron determination of these Jews. The other story is of the seven brethren. They were brought before Antiochus's men with their aged mother. They were given the choice of death by torture or of forsaking their beloved Law. The first was scourged and then broken on the wheel; the second had his skin torn from his head and then his flesh lacerated by men wearing gauntlets spiked with steel; the third was twisted on the rack and then flayed alive; the fourth had his tongue cut out; the fifth was fastened to a catapult and torn limb from limb; the sixth was burned and tortured with sharp, burning spits; the seventh was roasted in a gigantic frying pan; and the while their aged mother looked on and exhorted them to constancy (4 Mac. 8-13). They chose to die and so they died (1 Mac. 1:63). Never was there a people so tortured for their faith and never was there a people so resolute. Nothing could break their spirits.

The Liberators arise

In the end the liberators arose. In the little village of Modin there lived an aged priest called Mattathias who had five sons. Antiochus's men came to the village to compel sacrifice to the pagan gods. The leader suggested that Mattathias should show an example by sacrificing and so save the village from vengeance; he refused. Then a renegade Jew stepped forth and sacrificed. Mattathias in a holy rage leapt forward and killed him and then sprang upon Antiochus's commissioner and killed him, too. The standard of revolt was raised; there were battles in the mountains against incredible odds; but in the end Judas Maccabaeus, the son of Mattathias won liberty again for the Jews and cleansed the Temple which had been so terribly defiled. It would have been so easy in those dreadful days for the Jews to abandon their faith and to give in; but they held fast to it. What would have happened if the Jewish faith had been wiped out? God's plan would have been frustrated and he could not have sent his Son into Palestine. But the unwavering fidelity of the Jews stood fast for God and for their Law.

Things worth dying for

There are certain things which we may learn from these Jewish heroes. For one thing, they were sure that *there were things worth dying for*. They were sure that if they lost certain things life would not be worth living. One thing is always true in life. If we choose an easy way of escape from trouble, if we choose a cowardly safety we will regret it all our lives. We are so made that it makes us happier to do the right thing and to suffer for it than it does to choose a cowardly way and to escape trouble. If we want the highest kind of satisfaction and happiness we will find them only in one way—the way of doing the right thing. We have got a conscience and we can never get away from that conscience. We can take an easy way and we can escape trouble by being cowards; but if we do, our consciences will never let us alone and we will never be happy again. There is nothing that makes us happy like doing the right thing however hard the right thing may be.

Passing it on

Further, we learn this from these Jewish heroes—that, *if a man does the right thing it not only benefits him but it benefits people in all ages to come*. These Jewish heroes kept the faith and because they kept the faith the Jewish faith did not die but kept on burning brightly. In a very real sense they made it possible for Jesus to come. When a man does a fine thing he does not only bring honour to himself; he makes things easier for others in the days to come. In life we are all like links in a chain. If we are a strong link then the whole chain gains strength; if we are a weak link then the whole chain is weakened. When Latimer and Ridley were being burned in front of Balliol College in Oxford for their faith, Latimer turned to Ridley and said, "Be of good cheer, Master Ridley, and play the man; for this day we shall light such a candle in England as by God's grace will never be put out." He felt that they were doing something which was going to make things easier for others in the days to come. In America one of the great engineering feats was the building of Boulder Dam which brought water and fertility to an area which had been parched and barren. In the building of the dam there were men who in accidents lost their lives. When the dam was finished a tablet was let into it and on it there was written the list of those who had died and beneath it the words, "These died that the desert might rejoice and blossom as the rose." We owe all the precious things to men who in their day and generation were true and we must be true so that we can hand on the precious things to others.

In the Succession of the Prophets

Sometimes when we do the right thing and the straight thing it is bound to make us unpopular and it is bound to get us into trouble. When it is difficult and when it does make things hard for us, there is one thing which will help. At such a time we are doing the very thing the saints and the martyrs and the prophets did. We are walking in the way they walked. I remember once playing in a football match for a certain charity. A very famous team lent their strip for the occasion. Of course, the jerseys were numbered; and I remember yet the thrill I got when I pulled over my head the jersey that a certain famous Scottish international wore every Saturday. I was wearing the jersey of a great player. When we do the right thing and suffer something for it, it is just as if we were in the same team as the great prophets and the great martyrs. It should give us a real thrill to be treading where the saints have trod.

Faithful unto Death

In the terrible days of Antiochus Epiphanes the Jews were faithful unto death. They knew that there were certain things worth suffering for. They knew that they were not only bringing honour to themselves but that they were also making it easier for those who would come afterwards. They knew that they were taking the same way as the great heroes had taken. If we think of these things it will make it easier to do the right thing when the right thing is hard to do.

QUESTIONS FOR DISCUSSION

1. It is very unlikely that nowadays we will have to die for our faith. What is it that we may have to suffer, if we are absolutely true to our faith?

2. If it did become necessary, what things do you think are worth dying for?

3. Would you say that it is right to go to war to protect your religion? If not, how would you protect it?

13. THE END OF A NATION

(The period from 165 B.C. *until* A.D. 70 *is one of the most complicated periods of Jewish history. It is also obviously one of the most important because it is the time which is the immediate background of the life of Jesus and the rise of Christianity. Clearly it is impossible to study it in detail here. All we can do is to lay down its main lines and to glance at its most vivid moments. The following books will be found invaluable:*

"Judaism in the Greek Period," *Volume 5 of the Old Testament Section of the Clarendon Bible, by G. H. Box, Oxford University Press,* 1932;

"The Jews under Roman Rule," *by W. D. Morrison, T. Fisher Unwin,* 1890, *in the Story of the Nations Series;*

"A History of the Jewish People during the Maccabæan and Roman Periods," *by James Stevenson, Riggs Smith, Elder and Co.,* 1900;

and especially to be commended:

"The Jews from Cyrus to Herod," *by Norman H. Snaith, in the Gateway Handbooks of Religious Knowledge Series, The Religious Education Press Ltd.,* 1949.)

The Gallantry of the Maccabees

We have seen how in the dark days when Antiochus Epiphanes was trying to wipe out the Jewish religion there rose in the hill country Judas Maccabaeus and his brothers to defend the faith. Judas was one of five brothers. One by one they assumed the leadership; and one by one they fought and were killed; and Judas himself was one of the greatest generals and the greatest exponents of guerrilla warfare the world has ever seen. The name Maccabaeus very likely means *The Hammerer*, and in truth Judas was the hammer of the enemies of his country. Again and again with forces which seemed ridiculously and fantastically small he won impossible victories. We take but one example, the Battle of Emmaus in 166 B.C. At first the Syrians had thought that Judas would be easily beaten; but again and again Judas had swooped from the hills and devastated their armies and slipped through their hands before they could close in on him. But in

166 B.C. the Syrians determined to end this menace. They sent to Palestine an army of 40,000 foot and 7,000 horsemen under three first-class generals, Ptolemy, Nicanor and Gorgias. Judas had 3,000 men and in their poverty they were but ill-equipped. So sure were the Syrians of triumph that even merchants accompanied their army to buy as slaves the Jews whom they regarded as certain to be conquered. The Syrians knew where Judas was encamped and they sent Gorgias with 5,000 troops to attack the camp and to wipe out the Jews. They were actually led to the place by renegade and traitorous Jews. Judas got word of what was happening. Under cover of darkness he slipped out of the camp with his men though he left the camp fires burning to look as if the camp were still occupied. So when the Syrians descended on the camp they found it empty; they had no idea where Judas had gone so they set out to look for him. But Judas had planned the boldest of bold strokes. He had not gone into hiding; he had marched straight for the Syrian camp. His little army of three thousand lay concealed close to it. It looked a hopeless task for the gallant 3,000 to launch an attack on the remaining 42,000 Syrians. But down swooped Judas with his men. His trumpets sounded for the battle and the Jews charged with such fury and impetus that they put the Syrians into panic-stricken flight. They chased them out of the country and slew 3,000 of them and gained rich spoils. It was by exploits such as that that Judas showed himself a leader of men of the highest quality. In the end Judas died, but one by one his brothers carried on the fight.

Trouble comes

But trouble was soon to come. As we have seen this struggle began as a simple struggle for religious freedom and for existence. But as the years went on and the successes multiplied, it became something very different. It became a struggle not for freedom —that had been won long ago—but a struggle to found a new Jewish empire and to push the bounds of Jewish power as far as they could be pushed. Now this policy of conquest tore the nation in two. One section of the nation held that all that was wanted and all that God wanted was simply freedom to worship

God in their own way. They had won that and this party strongly disapproved of the policy of expansion. And they disapproved especially of the fact that the later Jewish leaders called themselves kings. The other party were a political party. They were all out for power and glory and empire. These two parties found their focus in two names which are exceedingly familiar to us. The party who simply wished to worship God in their own way and who were set against a policy of imperial conquest were the Pharisees. The political party who aimed at power were the Sadducees. And between these two parties the nation was torn in two. Not unnaturally it was the political party which was the more popular of the two. The thing came to a head in the reign of Alexander Jannaeus, who reigned from 101 until 75 B.C. Then actual civil war broke out. Finally, Alexander Jannaeus shut up the Pharisees in the village of Bethome. He captured them and brought them to Jerusalem. And then he did a terrible thing. As Josephus, the Jewish historian put it: "As he was feasting with his concubines, in the sight of all the city, he ordered about eight hundred of them to be crucified; and while they were still living, he ordered the throats of their children and wives to be cut before their eyes" (Josephus, *The Antiquities of the Jews*, Book 14, Chapter 14, Section 2). The struggle which had begun as a gallant fight for freedom had turned into a civil war in which Jew killed Jew with a terrible savagery.

Enter the Romans

And now there came the first of the events which, for the Jews, was the beginning of the final end. As anyone can see, Palestine was by this time in a state of utterly chaotic upheaval. At this time the masters of the world were the Romans. The Romans tried to settle the affairs of Palestine by peaceful means. They found it impossible and under Pompey, their great general, they invaded Palestine in 63 B.C. For three months Pompey besieged Jerusalem. When the Jews saw that it was hopeless many of them leaped to death over the Temple battlements into the ravine below; others set fire to their own houses and perished in the flames. But the end came. Pompey entered the Temple; he horrified the Jews by even entering the Holy of holies. He destroyed the walls of Jerusalem and Palestine became a Roman tributary kingdom. The Romans were in Palestine and they were never to go out again.

The Rise of Herod

The Romans did what they always did. They did not at first put in a Roman governor. The Romans always allowed their subject nations to govern themselves so long as good order was maintained and tribute paid. The name of the governor was Antipater. He was a good governor and he arranged things so well that the Romans actually allowed him to rebuild the walls of Jerusalem. But the Jews hated him because he came from Idumaea—which is the ancient Edom—and was therefore only half a Jew. One can only feel that a kind of terrible insanity had fallen on the Jewish nation. In 43 B.C. Antipater was assassinated and chaos again descended on Palestine. Antipater's son was Herod, who was to become Herod the Great. He fled to Rome without a penny to his name. Herod was in many ways a great man and the Romans knew it and they appointed him king. Galilee and Samaria accepted him, but Judaea would have nothing to do with the man they called "the Idumaean slave". In 37 B.C. the Romans sent an army to Palestine and made Herod king by force. By this time the Romans had lost all patience and in the fight in Jerusalem they slaughtered men, women and children alike while Herod vainly tried to stop them.

The Reign of Herod

For more than thirty years Herod reigned as king. In many ways he was a very great king. He was an excellent administrator and he was loyal to Rome. He was a great builder. He rebuilt the Temple in all its magnificence. He built the great seaport of Caesarea. He covered Jerusalem with magnificent buildings. He was generous to the people. When things were difficult for the common people in 20 B.C. he remitted a third of the taxes and in 14 B.C. a quarter. During a famine in 25 B.C. he melted down his own royal plate to buy corn from Egypt. But in his nature there was a queer vein of suspicion. He suspected everyone. Because of that his reign was scattered with assassinations. He murdered his wife Miriamne and her mother Alexandra. He murdered his sons, Alexander and Aristobulus, and on his death-bed arranged the assassination of his eldest son, Antipater. When he ordered the slaughter of the children in Bethlehem because he had heard that the king of the Jews was born there, he was acting strictly in character. When he was seventy he fell ill of a terrible disease. He went to Jericho to die and played one last grim jest. He ordered that all the most distinguished citizens of Jerusalem should be arrested on trumped-up charges and held in prison and that when he died they should all be executed. Grimly he said that he was well aware that when he died no one would shed tears for him and he was determined that tears should be shed for someone. So Herod died. Now for all his faults he had been a strong man who had kept the peace; and when he died Judaea erupted. Again this fanatical insanity of the Jews breaks out.

The Roman Procurators arrive

Herod had left his kingdom to three of his sons. To Herod Antipas he left Galilee and Peraea. Pilate sent Jesus to this Herod during his trial. To Philip he left Ituraea and Trachonitis and the wild region in the north-west. To Archelaus he left Judaea, Samaria and Edom. Now Herod Antipas and Philip settled in and settled down. But Archelaus was a weak and vicious character. Judaea was torn with revolt. Finally, the Jews sent a deputation to Rome asking for Archelaus to be removed. The Romans did remove him; but this time, tired of the Jews and their troublous ways, the Romans put into Judaea a procurator who was definitely and directly a Roman governor. Of these Roman governors, we meet in the New Testament Cyrenius, Felix, Festus, and—most famous of all— Pontius Pilate. So, in 6 B.C., Judaea lost the last remnants of her liberty and her independence.

The last Days

So we come to the last days and they were terrible days. The Jews were ill to govern. We cannot tell the whole story.

Rebellions were frequent. There was, for instance, a rebellion when Jesus was eleven years of age. It centred in Sepphoris, which was a city only four miles from Nazareth. The Romans dealt with it savagely and in revenge crucified 2,000 men on crosses all along the highway so that all might see the fate of those who rose against Rome. It was in these days that the Zealots arose. The Zealots were wild nationalists who were quite prepared to follow out a programme of assassination and crime to seek to drive the Romans from Palestine. At last the Romans lost all patience. The end came in A.D. 70. The Jews barricaded themselves on the Temple hill and the Temple had to be captured almost literally stone by stone. They held out until they were in such a state of starvation that they were actually practising cannibalism. But on the 6th September, A.D. 70, Jerusalem fell and the Romans destroyed it so completely that they drove a plough across the ruins. As a nation the Jews had come to an end; and their own mad folly had brought their end upon them.

Fighting against God

It has been cynically said that history is the record of the sins, the follies and the mistakes of men. And that is true of Jewish history. All this terrible story shows us three things. *It shows us what happens when men prefer their plans to God's plan.* The Jews destroyed themselves because they could not and would not accept the situation God had sent to them. If they had accepted the situation they could have lived useful lives serving their fellow men and serving God; but in the end they poured out their own blood and wrecked their country in useless battles and wars. When anything happens to us from which there is no escape the first thing to do is to accept it. Someone tells of an old negro who lived a very hard and difficult life, but who never complained and never grumbled and never grew angry. When they asked him his secret, he answered, "I learned to compromise with the inevitable." The Stoics believed that everything that happened to us was sent by God. They said that the way to peace was to accept it because God sent it. To resent it and resist it and fight against it was just like banging one's head against a brick wall; it was only to hurt oneself. Paul had had a vivid picture of himself before he accepted God's will. He said he was kicking against the pricks. When a young ox was yoked to a wagon he did not like it. So he tried to kick the wagon to bits. But in front of the wagon and behind his hind legs there was fixed a bar studded with wooden spikes and every time he kicked he only hurt himself until he learned to submit. If the Jews had only learned to accept things, what they might have done! Instead of fighting the Romans they might have converted them to the love and the service of the only true God. But because they would not accept it, they brought to the world battles instead of God. When we get involved in some situation which is difficult but which we cannot avoid, then we should say to ourselves not, How can I get out of this? but, How can I *use* this to improve myself and to help and serve others? There can be nothing but trouble when we will not give up our plans and accept God's plan for us.

The Degeneration of the Good

The most tragic thing about this whole story is how *something gallant and fine degenerated into something terrible*. It all began with the gallant fight of Judas Maccabaeus. That fight was won. Then the Jews mistakenly went on to fight for political power; and what had once been a gallant fight for freedom degenerated into an insane and fantastic series of selfish struggles. It is easy to degenerate. There is one man in the New Testament who is only mentioned three times, but he is a study in degeneration. His name was Demas. Paul mentions him three times. In Philemon 24 Demas is called Demas, my *fellow-labourer*. In Col. 4:14 he is just *Demas*. And in 2 Tim. 4:10 Paul writes, "Demas, in love with this present world, has deserted me." The man who was once the fellow-labourer is now the deserter. Demas is a study in degeneration. How it happened we will never know, but Demas started so well and ended so ill. It is told that when Leonardo da Vinci was painting his great picture of The Last Supper he looked for a model from which to paint the face of Jesus. He found a young man with a face so beautiful that he painted Jesus from him. The years passed on and he had one face left to paint. It was the face of Judas. He searched the lowest parts of the city until he found a man with a face so vicious and depraved and low that he knew he would serve as a model. When he had painted him the man said, "Sir, you painted me once before." Leonardo said, "I don't remember ever painting you." "Oh yes, you did," said the man, "and last time you painted me as Christ." What a degeneration was there. It is easy to degenerate. Our bodies degenerate unless we train them to keep fit. Our minds grow flabby unless we exercise them. We lose our skill in any game unless we practise. All the time we have got to be on the watch. All the time we have got to be asking Jesus to help in case we too begin well and finish ill.

The Coming of Hatred

Still further, all this story shows us that *when men desert God they hate each other*. This is a story of terrible wars and battles and cruelties. They would never have happened if men had obeyed God. In these days everyone dreads another war. We will never avoid war fully and finally by making treaties or even by piling up weapons. Men will only love each other if they love God. They will only be brothers of one another when they are all sons of God. If we want to make a safe world we must make a Christian world. We cannot affect the whole world, but we can affect the little bit of it where we live and work and play. We can help to get our own bit right by showing how men live when they live in complete obedience to God and in complete friendship with each other. And if all the bits are right then some day the whole world will be right, too, and men will be at peace with each other because they are true to God.

The End of a Nation

The Jewish nation came to a terrible end because men preferred their own plans to the plan of God; because a thing which was once a fine thing degenerated into a selfish and an evil thing; because they came to hate each other; because they did not really love God.

QUESTIONS FOR DISCUSSION

1. Of what does real national greatness consist?
2. Is there any such thing as a just war?
3. What kind of men should a nation's leaders be?

PART III

CONCEPTS OF THE KINGDOM

1. THE DREAM OF THE GOLDEN DAYS

The Kingdom of God

So far we have been thinking of the Kingdom of Israel. We have seen how it rose and how it fell in ruins. And now we are to turn our thoughts to another kingdom—the Kingdom of God. The Kingdom of God was the centre of Jesus' message. Mark tells us that Jesus came into Galilee telling forth the good news of the Kingdom of God (Mark 1:14, 15). All over the gospels this phrase, "the Kingdom of God" recurs. In one form or another this occurs 49 times in Matthew, 16 times in Mark and 38 times in Luke. Clearly Jesus spent much of his time speaking about this Kingdom of God. Now we must note one thing. When Jesus used this phrase right at the beginning of his ministry he did not stop to explain it; he used it in the full confidence that everyone would recognise it and would have at least some idea of what he was talking about. And that is so because every Jew dreamed of the Kingdom of God which was to come. There is a great wealth of meaning in this phrase and we will be studying it for many weeks to come, but right at the beginning there is something we must always remember about it. When we use the word *Kingdom* we usually mean a land, an area of territory, a part of the world. For instance, the Kingdom of Britain is the British Isles; the Kingdom of Belgium is an area and a territory in the continent of Europe. But when we use the phrase the *Kingdom of God* we mean the rule, the kingship, the dominion of God, not over any land or lands, but in men's hearts and in men's minds and in men's lives.

The Jewish Idea of the Kingdom

The idea of the Kingdom has a long and a fascinating history, and before we come to Jesus' own particular teaching about it we must look at what the Jews believed and how their ideas about it grew and changed and developed.Throughout all their days as a nation the Jews looked forward to a golden time that was to come. It is very interesting to note that the Jews did look *forward*. Far more commonly people looked back to the golden age. The Romans, for instance, looked back to a golden time when Saturn had been king; the Greeks looked back to a golden time when all the world had been young; even today we are apt to look back and to use phrases like "good Queen Bess's glorious days" as if all the great days had been in the past. In this the Jews were right. If we believe in God we must always be looking forward; we must always be sure that the best is still to be. It is one of the signs of a really Christian man that he does not look back and weep and wail and regret about the good old days; he looks forward, sure that just because God is always God, the best is always still to come. When David Livingstone desired to become a missionary the Society to which he offered his services asked him where he wanted to go. His answer was, "I am ready to go anywhere, *so long as it is forward*." The Jews were right always to have the forward look. The Jewish idea of the Kingdom was not by any means always the same. We must begin with the very first ideas they had about the golden age which God was going to bring some day into this world. We will get pictures of that golden age scattered all through the writings of the prophets and we are going to look at some of them now.

The Age of Plenty

For one thing, the golden age, the Kingdom of God to come, was to be an *age of plenty*. It was to be an age when the earth would bring forth her fruits in glorious abundance and when all men would have enough and more than enough and when none would have too little. Here are some of the dreams that the prophets had.

"Behold the days are coming," says the Lord, "when the ploughman shall overtake the reaper and the treader of grapes him who sows the seed; the mountains shall drip sweet wine, and all the hills shall flow with it. . . . They shall plant vineyards and drink their wine, and they shall make gardens and eat their fruit" (Amos 9:13, 14).

The land was to be so rich and fertile that the reaper would reap on the very heels of the man who sowed.

The wilderness becomes a fruitful field, and the fruitful field is deemed a forest (Is. 32:15).

God will comfort all her waste places, and will make her wilderness like Eden, her desert like the garden of the Lord (Is. 51:3).

The wilderness and the dry land shall be glad, the desert shall rejoice and blossom. . . . The burning sand shall become a pool, and the thirsty ground springs of water (Is. 35:1, 7).

They shall come and sing aloud on the height of Zion, and they shall be radiant over the goodness of the Lord, over the grain, the wine, and the oil, and over the young of the flock and the herd; their life shall be like a watered garden (Jer. 31:12).

So then the golden days were to be a time when none would be hungry and none would be thirsty and none would be poor any more.

We must always remember that God is interested in our bodies as well as in our souls. When Jesus was on this earth more than once he fed the hungry people because he was sorry for them. When General Booth began the Salvation Army he gave poor people free meals. He was criticised for that. People said that it was not part of the Church's duty to give men meals. Booth answered, "It is impossible to warm men's hearts with the love of God when their feet are perishing with cold." He meant that he considered it his duty not only to bring men wise words, but to bring them health and help and food when they were poor and hungry. This means something very practical. It means that the farmer and the ploughman and the gardener and the keeper of the orchard, the baker and the persons who cook our meals for us, are all just as really serving God as any minister of the Church. They are all helping God to work out His plan that men should have pure hearts and healthy bodies.

The Age of Friendship

One of the loveliest ideas about the golden days to come was that *the enmity between man and the beasts would no longer exist*. Even the beasts which are naturally savage and hostile to man would become tame and gentle. Here are some things the prophets have to say about that.

I will make for you a covenant on that day with the beasts of the field, the birds of the air, and the creeping things of the ground; and I will abolish the bow, the sword, and war from the land; and I will make you lie down in safety (Hos. 2:18).

The wolf shall dwell with the lamb, and the leopard shall lie down with the kid, and the calf and the lion and the fatling together, and a little child shall lead them. The cow and the bear shall feed; their young shall lie down together; and the lion shall eat straw like the ox. The sucking child shall play over the hole of the asp, and the weaned child shall put his hand on the adder's den. They shall not hurt or destroy in all my holy mountain (Is. 11:6-9).

The wolf and the lamb shall feed together, the lion shall eat straw like the ox. . . . They shall not hurt or destroy in all my holy mountain, says the Lord (Is. 65:25).

When Robert Burns, the great poet, turned up a little field mouse's nest with the plough, and when the little mouse ran terrified from him, Burns was sorry to see the tiny animal so frightened of him and he wrote:

> "I'm truly sorry man's dominion
> Has broken nature's social union."

He felt that man and the beasts had not been made to be afraid of each other or to be enemies of each other. Until the coming of the Christian faith men were terribly cruel to animals; they did not care how much suffering they caused them, often quite needlessly; they completely neglected to care for them. It is a terrible thing to ill-treat and ill-use a helpless dumb animal. Once R. L. Stevenson saw a man ill-treating a dog. He said to the friend he was with, "I'm going to stop him." The friend not wishing to be involved in a scene, said, "Why worry? It's not your dog." "I know," said Stevenson, "that it is not my dog, but it's God's dog and I'm not going to stand by and see it ill-treated." Coleridge wrote:

> "He prayeth best who loveth best
> All things both great and small."

There was a poet called Ralph Hodgson who loved all animals and who was very sorry when animals were ill-treated, and he wrote a little poem like this:

> " 'Twould ring the bells of heaven the wildest peal for years,
> If Parson lost his senses and people came to theirs,
> And he and they together knelt down with angry prayers,
> For tamed and shabby tigers, and dancing dogs and bears,
> And wretched, blind pit ponies, and little, hunted hares."

In the golden age there would arise a friendship which would cover all the earth.

The End of Pain

Still further, the prophets dreamed that in the golden days, *all the earth's pain would pass away.* A new strength and a new health would come into life. Here are some of the things the prophets foretold about that.

> No more shall there be in it an infant that lives but a few days, or an old man who does not fill out his days, for the child shall die a hundred years old (Is. 65:20).

We often speak of someone dying too young or being cut off too soon. In the golden days that would never happen. A man's life would be like the life of a tree for years (Is. 65: 22).

> No inhabitant will say, "I am sick" (Is. 33:24).

All illness was to be taken away and even death was to be vanquished.

> He will swallow up death for ever, and the Lord God will wipe away tears from all faces (Is. 25:8).

The dream of a world where there will be no more pain and age and weakness and decay is a wonderful dream. The Highlanders, in the Gaelic, call Heaven *Tir-nan-og*, The Land of the Ever Young; but in the golden days earth itself would be a place like that.

Once again this has the most practical consequences. Of course it means that all doctors and nurses are helping to bring in the golden days. Dr. Schweitzer, the great missionary doctor, said that one of the greatest thrills in life for him was when a native was brought in suffering from some agonizing pain or wound, and when he had operated, and when the man woke up and said in sheer amazement, "I have no more pain." No one is a truer servant of God than a good doctor and a kind nurse. It means that the scientist and the chemist who find new drugs and new cures are servants of God. It means that the dustman who takes away the refuse, the plumber who inspects the drains, the people who work on the sewage systems of villages and cities are all doing God's work because they are helping to eliminate infection and disease. It means that the scientist who makes new and wonderful instruments to help diagnose disease is a servant of God. It means that everyone who is helping to make a healthier and a happier world is working for and with God.

The Age of Peace

Lastly, the golden days were to be *an age of peace*, when war was finally stilled. Here are some of the things the prophets have to say about that.

> They shall beat their swords into ploughshares, and their spears into pruning hooks; nation shall not lift up sword against nation, neither shall they learn war any more (Is. 2:4).

> They shall not hurt or destroy in all my holy mountain (Is. 11:9).

> My people will abide in a peaceful habitation, in secure dwellings, and in quiet resting places (Is. 32:18).

Slowly men have come to see that there is nothing glorious about war. Long ago one of the great Greek dramatists wished to have a scene in one of his plays to show what war was like. He did not bring on armies in shining armour and with banners flying. He brought on an old woman bowed with sorrow and a bewildered little child. He wanted to show that war brings sorrow to the aged and makes the children orphans. A journalist tells how he discovered what war was. It was in the Spanish Civil War. He was driving through a Spanish city. He noticed, walking along the edge of a pavement, a little boy dragging a toy engine along by a string, a broken toy because the wheels had come off. Suddenly there was a burst of machine-gun fire and people scurried for safety. Then it was quiet again; the journalist looked back and the little boy was lying dead in the gutter, shot down. That is the kind of thing that war can do. The golden days, God's Kingdom, the prophets told us, will be days of peace. We can learn to be kind and to forgive and to live at peace and if we do so we will be helping on the golden days.

The Dream of the Golden Days

So even before Jesus came the Jews had their dreams of the Kingdom. It was to be a time of plenty when all men had enough and none too little. It was to be a time when even the animals and men lived in friendship. It was to be a time when there was peace over all the earth. And all that can only happen when God is king.

QUESTIONS FOR DISCUSSION

1. In view of these pictures of the Kingdom, which, do you think, is the place of the Social Gospel in the task of the Church?

2. What should the Church's attitude to war be?

3. Are the minister and parson the only people with a right to be called servants of God?

2. THE DREAM OF THE CHOSEN PEOPLE

God's chosen People

In our last chapter we saw something of the lovely dreams of the golden days that the prophets and the people of Israel had. Now in that golden world to come the Jews were always certain that they were to occupy a very special and a very important place. No matter what life was like, even when their national affairs were in disaster, even though they lived in so small a country and were so few in numbers, they never lost the consciousness of being in a very special way God's chosen people. Because of that they never doubted that they would enjoy a special and a peculiar place in the wonderful days to come when God's Kingdom came among men. But different people had different dreams of what that place would be; and now we must look at some of these different expectations which the Jews held about their place in the golden age to come.

Jerusalem the Centre of the World

Some of them thought that in the new world *Jerusalem would be the centre of the world, and that all the nations would come to it to learn the ways of God.* Here is how Isaiah told his dreams of that day.

> It shall come to pass in the latter days that the mountain of the house of the Lord shall be established as the highest of the mountains, and shall be raised above the hills; and all the nations shall flow to it, and many peoples shall come, and say: "Come, let us go up to the mountain of the Lord, to the house of the God of Jacob; that he may teach us his ways and that we may walk in his paths." For out of Zion shall go forth the law, and the word of the Lord from Jerusalem (Is. 2:2, 3; cp. Mic. 4:1, 2).

The idea was that by their obedience to God and by the help of God the Jews would be enabled to live a life so lovely and to build up a state and a city so perfect that all nations would see it and would come to learn the secret of that beauty and that goodness. This was a great dream. In essence it meant that the Jews believed that some day God would enable them to make the worship and the service of the true God so lovely a thing that all men everywhere would desire to have it and to share it. There is a great truth here. The only way in which we will ever persuade others to become Christians is not by talking about Christianity, but by living it. Very, very few people have been argued into Christianity. What has persuaded people to become Christians is the unanswerable evidence of a Christian life. If we, as Christians, can show those who are not Christians that we possess something that they have not got, then inevitably they will wish to share it. People will always listen to the man who can give them something which no one else can give. A great American thinker said, "If a man can make a better mousetrap than his neighbours men will make a beaten track to his door even if he lives in the middle of a wood." The trouble is that so often people have made of Christianity an unattractive thing. In the old days of the Spanish Inquisition when the Spaniards tried to torture people into being Christians, an incident like this happened in Central America. The Spaniards had captured one of the South American chiefs, one of the Incas. He knew how they tortured people with the rack and the thumbscrew and all the apparatus of torture to make them become Christians. They demanded that he should become a Christian or be tortured; they told him that if he did become a Christian he would go to heaven and if he did not he would go to hell. His answer was, "I will not become a Christian, because I would rather go to hell with my own people than go to heaven with people like you." These men made Christianity a horrible thing. If we want to help on the Kingdom of God we will live so bravely, so honestly, so kindly, so forgivingly, so helpfully, that men will see that we have a secret they do not possess and will want with all their hearts to share it. The Jews had a dream that some day they would make God's service and God's worship so lovely that all nations would come to Jerusalem to learn about this lovely thing. That was one of their noblest dreams.

A Light to the Gentiles

Some few of the Jews, some very few, had the dream that *the Jews must go out to all the world and bring to all men the knowledge and the love of God.* That is to say, they held that their nation had a missionary duty. Here is what Isaiah hears God saying to the nation.

I will give you as a light to the nations, that my salvation may reach to the end of the earth (Is. 49:6).

The glory of the Lord shall be revealed, and all flesh shall see it together (Is. 40:5).

This was the noblest and the best of all the dreams, but as we shall see it was a dream that only a very few of them ever had. If we have something very precious the really Christian thing is never to want to keep it to ourselves, but always to want to share it with others. In this the medical profession is our great example. If a doctor discovered a very valuable drug he could make a fortune by taking out a patent for it and so refusing to allow anyone else to use it. If a surgeon discovered some new technique which would make some hitherto impossible operation possible, and if he refused to allow anyone else to use the technique which he had discovered he could become colossally rich. But if a doctor discovered such a drug or if a surgeon discovered such a technique the first thing he would do would be to make it available to everyone so that as many people as possible might benefit from it. If ever medical science discovers a cure, for instance, for cancer, the discoverer of it could, if he kept it to himself, become the richest man in the world. But he will never do that; he will give it to all. Now it must be that way with our Christianity. When we discover how wonderful Jesus is the first thing that we must want to do is to tell everyone about Him. That is the way that Paul felt about it. F. W. H. Myers wrote a poem in one section of which he describes Paul's feelings when he thought of all the people who had never heard of Jesus Christ and in it he makes Paul say:

"Only like souls I see the folk thereunder
    Bound who should conquer, slaves who should be kings,—

Hearing their one hope with an empty wonder,
  Sadly contented in a show of things:
Then with a rush the intolerable craving
  Shivers throughout me like a trumpet call,—
Oh to save these! to perish for their saving,
  Die for their life, be offered for them all!"

His one desire was that all men should know and enjoy
what he knew and enjoyed.

There are some things which we can only keep by giving
away. There is a story of an old saint who made a pilgrimage
to a famous shrine. From the altar of the shrine he took a
light which he intended to carry back home with him so that
the very flame from the sacred altar should burn in his own
shrine. So he took the light and he carried it ever so carefully
that it might not go out. As he was travelling a poor woman
stopped him. Her fire had gone out; it was cold; it was long
before the days of matches and she had nothing wherewith to
rekindle it. She asked the saint for a flame from his light. At first
he refused; he would not share his precious and sacred light; but
in the end she persuaded him. He gave her the light and she
blessed him and he went on. So on he went and then he was
caught in a terrible blizzard of snow and wind. He did everything
to protect his light, but it was blown out and he was desolate.
Then he remembered that he had given the woman the light. If
he went back and kindled again his torch from her fire he would
still have fire from the sacred altar. So he went back and he
kindled his torch again at her fire; and as he did so he thought
how nearly he had refused to give her the light and he said to himself, "I would never have had my light unless I had given it away."
That is a parable of life. And it is specially true of our Christianity. Unless we share our Christianity, unless we give it to others,
we lose it. The noblest of all the Jewish dreams was that the Jews
were in the world to bring to all men the good news of God—
but it was tragically few of them who dreamed that dream.

The Dream of Power

There was a third dream that the Jews had of the great days
to come; and it was the dream of power. There were some who

dreamed that all the nations would come to Jerusalem to learn of God; there were some very few who dreamed that the Jews would go out to the Gentiles to teach them about God; but the vast majority of *the Jews dreamed that in the days to come the Jewish nation would become master and ruler of all the world.* They argued this way. They said, "We are God's chosen people; therefore, some day God is bound to exalt us above all other nations." They looked forward to a career of conquest which would finally bring every nation and all the world into subjection to the Jewish power. Here are some of the things they said about that dream.

> The nation and kingdom that will not serve you shall perish; those nations shall be utterly laid waste (Is. 60:12).

> The wealth of Egypt and the merchandise of Ethiopia, and the Sabeans, men of stature, shall come over to you and be yours, they shall follow you; they shall come over in chains and bow down to you (Is. 45:14).

> If any of the families of the earth do not go up to Jerusalem to worship the King, the Lord of hosts, there will be no rain upon them. And if the family of Egypt do not go up and present themselves, then upon them shall come the plague with which the Lord afflicts the nations that do not go up to keep the feast of booths (Zech. 14:17, 18).

This dream was a dream of world power in which the other nations would either be wiped out or would be brought in chains and in captivity to Jerusalem. It was the tragedy of the Jews that it was this dream of world power which really dominated their thoughts. They thought of themselves as God's chosen people, and so they were. But the question is—chosen for what? There are two ways of being chosen. A man can be chosen for special *privilege*, or he can be chosen for special *responsibility*. He can be chosen to have things done for him, or he can be chosen to do things for others. It was for responsibility and for service that God had chosen his people. But they never understood. It was their idea that all the other nations existed to serve them, while God had intended that they should exist to serve all other nations. That is why so few of them ever understood Jesus. Jesus said,"Let him who would be great be the servant of all" (Mark 10:43), but their dream was not to be the servant but the master of all.

History proved that they took the wrong way, because as a nation the Jews perished, while Jesus, the servant of God and the servant of men, is still the greatest figure in the world. If we want to be great we must learn to serve. It is the plain fact of all history that it is those who were the great servants of men who won true fame and whom men remember with honour. The real and the fine ambition is to do and give as much for others as we can. It is not the man who tries to rule others, but the man who tries to serve others who is the true servant of God. It is true that we are chosen, but the honour for which we are chosen is to go about doing good.

Someone wrote a poem in which he compared Jesus with the great conquerors who are half-forgotten while he shines the same as ever after all these centuries.

> "I saw the conquerors riding by,
>   With cruel lips and faces wan,
> Musing on kingdoms sacked and burned,
>   There rode the Mongol, Genghis Khan.
>
> And Alexander, like a god,
>   Who sought to weld the world in one;
> And Caesar with his laurel wreath,
>   And like a thing from hell, the Hun.
>
> And leading, like a star, the van,
>   Heedless of outstretched arm and groan,
> Inscrutable Napoleon went,
>   Dreaming of Empire and alone.
>
> Then all they perished from the scene,
>   As fleeting shadows on a glass,
> And conquering down the centuries came
>   Christ, the swordless, on an ass."

The Dreams of the chosen People

So the Jews dreamed their dreams of their place in the golden age that was to come. Some of them dreamed of a time when all men would come to Jerusalem to learn of God. Some of them, some very few, dreamed of a time when the Jews would go out and tell all men of God. But the vast majority dreamed of world power, and so failed to recognise the King of Love when He came to earth seeking a throne within the hearts of men.

QUESTIONS FOR DISCUSSION

1. How can a man be the servant of other men?
2. How can a nation be the servant of other nations?
3. What is the connection between political action and religion?

3. THE INTERVENTION OF GOD

The Coming of the golden Age

We have seen how the Jews never lost their dream of a golden age to come. And we have seen how that dream crystallised into the idea of a time when the Jews, God's chosen people, would be masters of the whole world and when all other nations would be wiped out or would become subject to them. How was that day to come? How was that dream ever to be realised?

The King of David's Line

In regard to this coming of the golden age there were two quite definite stages in the thought of the Jews. When we look at these two stages we must remember that the first of them never wholly passed away; but bit by bit the second became ever more dominant and widespread. At first the Jews believed that the golden age would come under the leadership and the guidance of some great king of David's line whom God would raise up. Here are some of the things that some of the Jewish thinkers said about the king who was to come from the house of David.

> Of the increase of his government and of peace there will be no end, upon the throne of David, and over his kingdom, to establish it, and to uphold it with justice and with righteousness from this time forth and for evermore (Is. 9:7).

> There shall come forth a shoot from the stump of Jesse, and a branch shall grow out of his roots (Is. 11:1).
>
> Then there shall enter the gates of this house kings who sit on the throne of David (Jer. 22:4).
>
> They shall serve the Lord their God and David their king, whom I will raise up for them (Jer. 30:9).
>
> Behold, the days are coming, says the Lord, when I will raise up for David a righteous Branch, and he shall reign as king and deal wisely, and shall execute justice and righteousness in the land (Jer. 23:5).

The Jews always looked back to the days of David as the greatest days of their national history and they always felt that if ever a really great age was to come it would be a king of David's line who would introduce it and who would reign over it. In Britain, our own country, we look back on the great days of Queen Elizabeth; and in our own time when another Elizabeth came to the throne one of the hopes that was much spoken about was that a new *Elizabethan Age* would come to our land. Just like that the Jews looked forward to a new Davidic kingdom when all the glory would come back and an even greater glory dawn.

When we read the New Testament we see that there were people who thought that Jesus was that son of David who would bring in the new greatness. When the blind man shouted out for Jesus' help near Jericho, he said, "Jesus, *Son of David* have mercy on me!" (Luke 18:38). When Jesus came riding into Jerusalem at his Triumphal Entry the crowds shouted, "Hosanna to the *Son of David!*" (Matt. 21:9). They believed that Jesus was the son of David who was to bring in the new age and make the nation great. They were right because Jesus was indeed the son of David who was to bring in the Kingdom; but they were also wrong because the Kingdom was not a political kingdom, but a reign of love within the hearts of men.

The Intervention of God

But although that idea of the king of David's line never died out, another idea of how the Kingdom was to come was far more dominant in Jewish thought. Think of the situation of the Jewish nation in actual fact. Their territory was never more than 120 miles from north to south and less than 50 miles from east to west. In numbers they were only a handful of people. They were surrounded on every side by vast empires with thousands and thousands of miles of territory and with millions upon millions of people. And yet they were God's chosen people and they were convinced that some day they must be masters of the earth. Even their own little kingdom split in two. Worse, there came exile and captivity. Freedom was gone; they were in turn the servants and the subjects of the Assyrians, the Babylonians, the Persians, the Greeks and the Romans. Slowly they began to see one thing completely clearly. By human means and by human power their hopes could never come true and the universal kingdom they dreamed of could never come. It was just incredible that by human means their little kingdom could ever master the world. And so another view began to dawn upon them. They began to dream that some day God would break directly into history; that God himself with all his power and might would arrive, as it were, personally on the scene, and would sweep their enemies away and make them masters of the world. What they with their resources could never do, God would do directly for them by superhuman and by divine means. That was the dream which dominated their hearts, that sooner or later God would himself descend into the arena of human history and smash their enemies and exalt them to world power.

The two Ages

Bit by bit they began to work out this dream. Now when we look at the way in which they worked out their dream we must remember that they are describing it in pictures; they are talking of it in poetry; they are trying to put into words dreams and visions which no words can express. We are not always to take everything strictly literally because it is dreams and visions that we are dealing with. But for all that certain broad lines emerge. First and foremost, they divided all time into two ages. There was the *The Present Age* and *The Age to Come*. The Present Age was wholly bad and wholly evil; the Age to Come was the golden age of God, the Kingdom which was altogether lovely and good. In between the two ages they put what they called *The Day of the Lord*. That phrase, *The Day of the Lord*, or sometimes simply *The Day* or *That Day*, occurs again and again in the Bible. The Day of the Lord was to be a day of utter terror and utter destruction. It was to be like the desperate birth-pangs of a new age. The scheme of things they had in mind was that the Present Age was wholly bad; to end it there would come this Day of the Lord which would be a day of shattering terror; and then there would be born the new golden age when God would reign and Israel rule supreme. That was the idea which Jesus would hear about when he was a boy. If we really want to see what the Jewish idea of the Kingdom was like, the idea which was in men's minds when Jesus came to the world, we must look at all this more closely.

The Day of the Terror

First and foremost, *they looked on the Day of the Lord as a day of destruction and terror*. Here are some of the things that they said about it.

> Behold the day of the Lord comes, cruel, with wrath and fierce anger, to make the earth a desolation and to destroy its sinners from it (Is. 13:9).

> Alas for the day! For the day of the Lord is near, and as destruction from the Almighty it comes (Joel 1:15).

> Blow the trumpet in Zion; sound the alarm on my holy mountain! Let all the inhabitants of the land tremble, for the day of the Lord is coming, it is near, a day of darkness and gloom, a day of clouds and thick darkness (Joel 2:1 and 2).

> Woe to you who desire the day of the Lord! Why would you have the day of the Lord? It is darkness, and not light. . . . Is not the day of the Lord darkness, and not light, and gloom with no brightness in it? (Amos 5:18-20).

> A day of wrath is that day, a day of distress and anguish, a day of ruin and devastation, a day of darkness and gloom, a day of clouds and thick darkness (Zeph. 1:15-16).

The picture of the coming of God is a picture of terror. Here the Jews had hold of something which was half true. It is true that there is such a thing as the fear of God. Fear can often be a very useful thing. Once the captain of a whaling ship was taking on new members for his crew. The work in these whaling ships which hunt the whales and shoot harpoons into them is very dangerous, for a whale maddened with pain could easily charge the ship and wreck it. He said, "I want no man on this ship who is not afraid of whales." He wanted no men who did not realise the danger and appreciate how great it was. We must feel that way about life. In a very real sense we must fear to disobey God for the consequences of such disobedience can be very terrible. But the God that Jesus taught us about is not a God of destruction but a God of love; His desire is not to destroy, but to save. The fear of the Jews was the terror of God's might and God's power and God's vengeance. Our fear must be the fear to hurt that love which loved us so much.

The sudden Coming

Secondly, the Jews were convinced that *this Day of the Lord would descend on the world without any warning whatever*. This is an idea which we find re-echoed in the New Testament.

The day of the Lord will come like a thief in the night (1 Thess. 5:2).
But the day of the Lord will come like a thief (2 Peter 3:10).

They believed that the day when God intervened and broke into history would come suddenly upon men.

This was a very wise and very valuable note to sound, because it means that always we have to be in readiness for the coming of God. One of the old saints used to say, "Live every day as if it were your last." That means that there must be nothing left half done or undone. Let us ask this question: if we do not know when God will come, if we cannot tell when life will end for us, how would we like God to find us? There is only one answer to that. The best way in which God could find us would be when we were quietly, faithfully and diligently going on with our work. A man's highest ambition should be that God should find him doing his job well. There is a negro spiritual like this:

> "There's a king and captain high,
> And he's coming by and by.
> And he'll find me hoeing cotton when he comes.
> You can hear his legions charging in the region of the sky,
> And he'll find me hoeing cotton when he comes.
> There's a man they thrust aside,
> Who was tortured till he died,
> And he'll find me hoeing cotton when he comes.
> He was hated and rejected,
> He was scorned and crucified,
> And he'll find me hoeing cotton when he comes.
> When he comes! When he comes!
> He'll be crowned by saints and angels when he comes.
> They'll be shouting out Hosanna! to the man that men
>   denied,
> And I'll kneel among my cotton when he comes."

The man who wrote that felt that God could best find him doing his day's work. A very great scholar and preacher once wrote: "Today I have a committee meeting, tomorrow I must lecture, on Sunday I must preach; some day I must die; well then, we must try to do each duty as it comes to us as well as we can." The Jews were right to warn us that we never can tell when God will come, but the man who faithfully goes on doing his day's work as it should be done need never be afraid.

The Shattered World

Thirdly, the Jews believed that at the Day of the Lord *this world, this whole universe would be shattered to pieces*. It is that idea of the world shaken and shattered and disintegrated which gives us some of the weirdest and most terrible pictures in the Bible. Here are some of them.

> But the day of the Lord will come like a thief, and then the heavens will pass away with a loud noise, and the elements will be dissolved with fire, and the earth and the works that are upon it will be burned up (2 Peter 3:10).

And I will give portents in the heavens and on the earth, blood and fire and columns of smoke. The sun shall be turned to darkness, and the moon to blood, before the great and terrible day of the Lord comes (Joel 2:30, 31).

For the stars of the heavens and their constellations will not give their light; the sun will be dark at its rising and the moon will not shed its light. . . . Therefore I will make the heavens tremble, and the earth will be shaken out of its place, at the wrath of the Lord of hosts in the day of his fierce anger (Is. 13:10, 13).

Between the Old and the New Testament Jewish writers and thinkers wrote many books in which they set down their dreams and visions of this terrible time that was to come upon the world before it was remade. When Jesus was a boy he would read those books and he would know those ideas. They got more and more terrible, but we must always remember, as we have already said, that they are dreams and visions, they are attempts to put into words things that are beyond words, and they are not to be taken literally, because the pictures of poetry are always pictures. Here are just two of them from among very many.

> And honour shall be turned into shame,
> And strength humiliated into contempt,
> And probity destroyed,
> And beauty shall become ugliness. . .
> And envy shall rise in those who had not thought aught of themselves,
> And passion shall seize him that is peaceful
> And many shall be stirred up in anger to injure many,
> And they shall rouse up armies in order to shed blood,
> And in the end they shall perish together with them
> (2 Baruch 27).

From heaven shall fall fiery swords down to the earth; Lights shall come, bright and great, flashing into the midst of men; and earth, the universal mother, shall shake in those days at the hand of the Eternal; and the fishes of the sea and the beasts of the earth and the countless tribes of flying things and all the souls of men and every sea shall shudder at the presence of the Eternal and there shall be panic. And the towering mountain peaks and the hills of the giants he shall rend and the murky abyss shall be visible to all. And the high ravines in the lofty mountains shall be full of dead bodies and rocks shall flow with blood and each torrent shall flood the plain . . . and God shall judge all with war and sword and there shall be brimstone from heaven, yea stones and rain and hail incessant and grievous. And death shall be upon the fourfooted beasts. . . . Yea the land itself shall drink of the blood of the perishing and beasts shall eat their fill of flesh (The Sibylline Oracles 3:263ff).

These are terrible pictures of what was to happen at the Day of the Lord, and we must remember that they are only pictures; but they do contain one great truth—this world as it stands is not fit to receive God; this world as it is just now is too evil a place for God to enter. Before God's Kingdom can come this world must be purified and renewed. Just think—how do we feel when we think of God entering into some city slum where people live in terrible conditions? How do we feel when we think of God entering into some of these places where people do and are encouraged to do the most wicked and immoral things? There are a great many places in this world into which we can only think of God entering with a shudder. There are evils to be rooted out before God's Kingdom can come. And every evil thing we can help to put away and to cure brings the coming of God nearer. All this confronts us not only with a warning, but with a task to do. God's world must be cleansed for the coming of God.

The Time of Judgment

Fourthly, the Jews believed that *this Day of the Lord would be a day of judgment*.

I will punish the world for its evil, and the wicked for their iniquity; I will put an end to the pride of the arrogant, and lay low the haughtiness of the ruthless (Is. 13:11).

Now in this thought of judgment there were many of the Jews who had a quite wrong idea. They believed that the judgment would fall only on the Gentiles and that they themselves were quite safe and quite immune. We get echoes of that in passages like Ez. 30:1-9 and in Zech. 14:1-3 where the punishment of the Gentiles and their nations is pictured. There were some Jews who believed in what we might call a more favoured nation clause. They were God's chosen people. Terrible judgments might fall on other nations, but they were quite safe—so they thought; God would never touch them. But there was one prophet who saw very clearly that things were not like that. His name was Amos. The first two chapters of his book give a long list of the punishments that will fall on other nations—on Gaza, Tyre, Edom, Ammon, Moab. Now the message of Amos was spoken long before it was written down and therefore these chapters were a sermon. When the listeners heard this they would agree thoroughly. They would be moved to applause and even to shouting out their agreement. Let the other nations be swept away in judgment! That was fine! But then suddenly Amos moves on to the Jews themselves. First of all he lists all the privileges the Jews have enjoyed. This was still fine! Were not they the chosen people? And then (Amos 3:2) there comes the sudden shattering statement, "You only have I known of all the families of the earth; therefore I will punish you for all your iniquities." The very fact that the Jews were the chosen people, the very fact that they had all kinds of special privileges and special favours and special treatment made their sins all the worse and their judgment all the more certain. Here again is a very great truth. It is certain that some day God will call us to account for all that we have said and done; and the better the chance we had to know the right and to do it, the harder will be our punishment if we have failed. But once again let us remember that we ought to think of this not only with fear. Suppose someone we admire and love gives us a job to do. Suppose that because we are careless and thoughtless we fail in that job and fall down on it. If that is so the thing that hurts most is not any punishment that comes to us; the thing that hurts most is the fact that we have disappointed someone who trusted us and whom we love. If we really love God the thing we will fear most of all is to disappoint him who loves us so much.

The golden Age

Fifthly and lastly, as we have already seen, the Jews believed
that after this Present Age had passed, after the terror of the
Day of the Lord, *there would come the golden time of the Age
to Come*. We have already seen many of the pictures in the Old
Testament of that wonderful time. Here is one from one of the
books between the Old and the New Testament and it is a
picture which Jesus must have known and read.

And then shall healing descend in dew,
And disease shall withdraw,
And anxiety and anguish and lamentation pass from
amongst men,
And gladness proceed through the whole earth.
And no one shall die untimely,
Nor shall any adversity suddenly befall.
And judgments and revilings and contentions and
revenges,
And blood and passions and envy and hatred,
And whatsoever things are like these shall go into con-
demnation when they are removed.
For it is these very things which have filled this world
with evils,
And on account of these the life of man has been greatly
troubled.
And the wild beasts shall come from the forest and
minister unto men,
And asps and dragons shall come forth from their holes
to submit themselves to a little child.
And women shall no longer then have pain when they bear
Nor shall they suffer torment when they yield the fruit of
the womb.
And it shall come to pass in those days that the reapers
shall not grow weary.
Nor those that build be toilworn,
For the works shall of themselves speedily advance
Together with those who do them in much tranquility,
For that time is the consummation of that which is
corruptible,
And the beginning of that which is not corruptible.

Therefore those things which were predicted shall belong
to it;
Therefore it is far away from evils, and near to the
things which die not.
This is the bright lightning which came after the last dark
waters (2 Baruch 73:1-74:4).

This is indeed a lovely picture. And once again here we have
a great truth—life can never be lovely and the world can never
be lovely until life and the world are cleansed and until God is
enthroned as King; and we can bring the lovely time a little
nearer by making God *our* Master and *our* King.

QUESTIONS FOR DISCUSSION

1. What are the privileges that we as individuals and as a
    nation have received and what are the responsibilities that
    are laid upon us?

2. How ought we to live if it is true that the end of life or the
    end of the world can come at any time?

3. What are the main evils in the civilisation in which we live?

4. WHAT JESUS MEANT BY THE KINGDOM

The Kingdom that is different

We have now traced the Jewish idea of the Kingdom of God;
and we have seen that, though a few of them had nobler and
higher ideals, to the great majority of the Jews, the Kingdom of
God meant a time when God would break into history and
subject every nation to the Jews so that Jerusalem would be the
capital of the world and every nation would admit Jewish
sovereignty. Now we must go on to what is far more important;
we must try to discover what Jesus meant when he spoke of the
Kingdom of God. Of one thing we may be quite sure, he did not
mean what the great majority of his fellow-countrymen meant.
When Jesus stood before Pilate, accused of claiming to be a

king, Pilate asked him, "Are you the king of the Jews?" (John
18:33). Jesus did not deny his claims to be king, but went on
to say, "My kingdom is not of this world" (John 18:36). To
Jesus the Kingdom was not a thing of power and force and
armies and battles and palaces and riches. Jesus' idea of the
Kingdom was quite different from the ideas that the world had.

The Will of God

If we are going to discuss anything we are always better to
start with an authoritative definition of what it is. Now Jesus
never defined the Kingdom in so many words; but once he
said something that shows quite clearly and unmistakably
what he believed the Kingdom to be. We call the prayer that
Jesus taught us to pray the Lord's Prayer. In that prayer
there are two petitions side by side—Thy kingdom come; thy
will be done in earth as it it is heaven. The Jews had a
characteristic way of saying everything twice. They said a thing
and then they repeated it in a way that developed it or brought
out the meaning of it or stated it in another way. If we want to
see this Jewish way of speaking in action we see it best of all
in the Psalms. In almost every verse of every psalm there is a
division in the middle; and the second half of the verse repeats,
develops or interprets the first part. Take, for example, two
verses from Psalm 46. In verse 1 the first half is *God is our
refuge and strength;* the second half is *a very present help in
time of trouble.* In verse 7 the first half is *The Lord of hosts is
with us;* the second half is *the God of Jacob is our refuge.* We
see how in each case the second half of the verse develops and
explains the first. We see Jesus using exactly the same way of
speaking in a verse like Matt. 10:24. The first half of the verse
is, *A disciple is not above his teacher;* the second half is, *nor a
servant above his master.* There again the second half of the
verse repeats the first half in a different way. Now we return
to the two petitions that Jesus taught us to pray. The first is
Thy Kingdom come; the second is, *Thy will be done in earth as
it is in heaven.* Remember that in the normal Jewish way of
speaking the second half will amplify and explain and develop
the first. So then when we put these two petitions together we

get a perfect definition of the Kingdom—*The Kingdom of God is a society and a state of things when God's will is as perfectly done on earth as it is in heaven.* Jesus' idea of the Kingdom was the idea of a time when all men would perfectly do the will of God. To Jesus the Kingdom meant not wealth or power or political prestige, but perfectly doing the will of God. To Jesus, to be a member of the Kingdom was not to be the master of men, but to be the perfect servant of God.

Past, Present and Future

This explains something which might puzzle us when we study the New Testament closely. It seems, at a first reading, strange that in the New Testament Jesus talks of the Kingdom as if it were at one and the same time past, present and future. In Matt. 8:11 (cp. Luke 13:28) he speaks of Abraham, Isaac and Jacob as being in the Kingdom of God. So then the Kingdom must have existed for long if Abraham, Isaac and Jacob are in it. In Luke 17:21 Jesus says, "The Kingdom of God is among you, or, within you." Scholars are not certain which is the right translation; but, whichever it is, it means that the Kingdom of God is here present now. In the Lord's Prayer itself, as we have been seeing, he bids us to pray, Thy Kingdom come. So then the Kingdom is something which is still to come and for which we must ever pray. How can the Kingdom be past, present and future at one and the same time? Let us go back to our definition. The Kingdom is a state when all men shall perfectly do the will of God. That means that no matter when a man lived, lives or will live, if he perfectly does God's will he is a member of God's Kingdom. Anyone who in the past perfectly did God's will is within the Kingdom; everyone who does it today is within the Kingdom; but the day has not yet come when all men everywhere do God's will and therefore the full and final coming of the Kingdom is still to come.

The Kingdom and I

This makes the whole matter of the Kingdom a personal one. It means that when we perfectly do God's will we become members of the Kingdom. It means that when we do our best to do so and ask God's help to do so, for we can never do it by ourselves, we are bringing nearer the day when all men shall be within the Kingdom. We have only to think how the great men spoke. When God spoke to Samuel, Samuel answered, "Speak for thy servant hears" (1 Sam. 3:10). When Jesus met Paul on the Damascus road, Paul said, "Lord, what do you want me to do?" (Acts 22:10). The Psalmist said, "I delight to do thy will, O God" (Ps. 40:8). "Teach me to do thy will," he said (Ps. 143:10). Jesus Himself said, "My food is to do the will of him who sent me" (John 4:34). "I seek not my own will but the will of him who sent me" (John 5:30). "I have come down from heaven, not to do my own will but the will of him who sent me" (John 6:38). It is always the same, the great men were great, Jesus was Jesus, they were members of the Kingdom and he was the head of the Kingdom, because they did the will of God. So then, as we have said, this becomes a personal thing. A Chinese Christian once prayed, "Lord, revive Thy Church, *beginning with me*." We might change that prayer just a little and pray, "Lord Jesus, bring in Thy Kingdom *beginning with me*." When we give our lives to Jesus in sincere faith and humble obedience we, too, become members of the Kingdom and we bring nearer the day when all the world will be the Kingdom of God.

The Voice of the Will of God

We may well go on to ask now, "How can we find out what is the will of God for us? How can we find out what God wants us to do?" There are many ways of finding out. First, we find out God's will *from the voice of conscience speaking within us*. We know quite well when we are about to do something which we should not do. A voice inside tells us to stop. We know quite well when there is something we ought to do. A voice inside us urges us constantly to go and do it. Once when one of the great saints was nearly going to do something that was wrong, he said, "The great God met me standing like a lion in my path." God stopped him doing it. The Stoics used to say that man's soul was what they called a spark of God dwelling in man's body. Our conscience is God speaking within us. Conscience tells us God's will; we must never disobey it.

The Voice of the Saints

Next, we learn God's will *from the advice, the counsel and the rebuke of good and godly people*. Someone has said that a saint is someone in whom Christ lives again. We all know people who are good and kind and wise and loving so that they have the reflection of Jesus upon them. We know people who give us good advice, who tell us what to do and who stop us doing silly and foolish and even wicked things. These people are God's voice to us. In his old age Thomas Carlyle used to say that even yet across the years from the graveyard in Ecclefechan his mother's voice came to him saying, "Trust in God and do the right." When wise and good people give us advice and warning we should never thoughtlessly reject it for that is God telling us his will.

The Voice of the Church

Next, we learn God's will *from God's Church*. When we worship in Church God's will is spoken to us. If the preacher is a real man of God he is bringing us God's word. Leslie Weatherhead tells of a boy who decided to become a minister of the gospel. Someone asked him when he had decided. He said it was after a certain service in his school chapel. He was asked who the preacher was. His answer was that he did not know the preacher's name, but he knew for sure that God had spoken to him that day. If we listen in Church reverently and intently, if we come prepared to take the guidance we will receive, God, through his Church, will tell us of his will.

The Voice of God's Book

Next, we learn God's will *from God's Book*. If we read our Bible we will find in it the kind of life God wants us to live and the kind of things he wants us to do and the kind of things he forbids us to do. In 1639, in America, the colony of New Haven was founded. The people began by meeting together to decide what kind of rule and government they would have. John Davenport rose and put the resolution that the Scriptures "do hold forth a perfect rule for the direction and government of men in all duties." There may be sections of the Bible which we do not understand; but there is enough that we do understand to make it quite clear what God wants us to do. If we read God's Book we will find God's will for us.

The Voice of Prayer

Next, we learn God's will *from prayer*. Prayer is just talking to God. When we are in doubt as to what to do then we ought to go to God and ask him. There is just one thing to remember about this. We should pray to God to make us humble and obedient enough to do what he tells us when we do pray to him. A great many people when they ask for advice only want the person they ask to agree with them and to tell them that they are quite right and to go ahead. If they are given advice that they do not want to take they get angry and go away annoyed. If we pray to God he will tell us the right thing to do; but to know the right thing is far from necessarily to do the right thing. We must not only ask for God's guidance; we must ask for humble obedience to accept it and for strength to do it.

The Voice of Jesus himself

Last and greatest of all, we will learn God's will *from Jesus himself*. Jesus, as we have said again and again, is not a figure in a book; he is a person who is alive and present with us all the time. There is a great legend which tells how once Peter met Jesus when Peter was about to do something very wrong. It was in Rome. Peter had been arrested and Peter's courage failed him and he escaped and ran away. As he was hastening down the Appian Way a figure met him, standing in his path. He looked up; it was Jesus himself. "Lord," said Peter, "whither goest thou?" "Peter," said Jesus, "I am going to Rome to be crucified again in your stead." And Peter shamed into heroism, turned back and did the right thing and died for his Master. Jesus is always with us; we can meet him every day, and every day he walks with us to tell us the will of God and to tell us what to do.

Right with God

And now we must ask still another question. Suppose we do the will of God with God's help, what will life be like? What will the consequences be for life? Will it not be a terrible struggle and often very unpleasant always to be having to do God's will? Paul has something very great and wise to tell us about this. In a very great verse he said, "The Kingdom of God . . . is *righteousness, peace* and *joy* in the Holy Spirit" (Rom. 14:17). First, then, this doing of God's will will mean *righteousness*. We must be very careful of the meaning of that word. It does not mean goodness because none of us can ever be perfect in the sight of God. We are only human beings and God is God, and just because of that all we could ever do would never be enough to make us good in the sight of God's perfection. *Righteousness means being right with God.* An old saint prayed a very lovely prayer. "O God," he said, "there is nothing between us." We know how when we have done something wrong at home there is a kind of barrier, an uncomfortable feeling, an invisible wall between us and our parents until we get things put right again. If we dedicate our lives by God's help to do God's will then there will be no barrier, no strangeness between us and God. We will never be afraid of God; we will always be able to think of God as the one to whom we can go any time, our best and truest friend.

Peace of Mind

Further, it will give us *peace of mind*. We can never have peace when we do wrong things. To put it at its lowest we will always be afraid that we will be found out. A famous writer in a book drew a picture of a man who had done a wrong thing. After he had done it the man lived in a wretchedly unhappy world. He said that the stars had it in their twinkling, the wind had it in its sighing, the trees had it in their rustling. The whole world became, as it were, his enemy. Apart altogether from the fear of being found out, we are so made that we cannot do wrong things, we cannot go against the will of God, and be happy. A wise man put it this way: in doing *his* will is *our* peace. Doing the will of God can be hard, but it is the way of peace.

The real Joy

Lastly, it will bring us *joy*. There is only one real joy. There is a certain kind of joy in having a good time and in doing what we like; but the deepest joy of all is to do a difficult and a hard job and to bring it to a successful conclusion. We do not need even to be successful; it will be enough to have done our best. There was a famous musician called Rossini. He wanted to get rich quick and he sometimes wrote very cheap and poor music. Once one of his pieces was being produced; he was happy because there was a big crowd and he was popular, although he knew it was a cheap thing; and then he caught a glimpse of Verdi, the greatest musician of the day, "sitting patient in his stall." He knew that Verdi, the master, saw through the applause and the popularity and saw how trivial the thing was; and suddenly Rossini was wretched. We never get real joy out of a cheap and easy performance in life. We get it only out of honestly trying by God's help to do God's will, by being loyal and true citizens of the Kingdom.

Jesus' Idea of the Kingdom

So, then, to Jesus, the Kingdom is a society on earth where God's will is as perfectly done as it is in heaven. When we do God's will by God's help we are in the Kingdom. We find that will through the voice of conscience, through the words of godly people, through the Church, through the Bible, through prayer and from Jesus himself. To do God's will may be hard and difficult, but in the end it is the way to being a friend of God, to the deepest peace of mind and to real joy.

QUESTIONS FOR DISCUSSION

1. Most people think of prayer as *talking* to God: but, if we are to know God's will, prayer must be equally *listening* to God. How can we make it so?

2. When we get a "message", how can we be sure that it is the voice of God and not just our own wishes and ideas?

3. What difficulties may doing the will of God involve?

5. OF SUCH IS THE KINGDOM OF GOD

Passports to the Kingdom

We have seen that the Kingdom is a state of things when God's will is as perfectly done on earth as it is in heaven. We have seen that this becomes a personal thing and that when a man does God's will by God's help he has the great privilege of being a citizen of the Kingdom. We must now look at the kind of things a man must do and the kind of things a man must be if he is so to do God's will and if he is to enter the Kingdom. We could call these things the conditions of citizenship of the Kingdom, or passports to the Kingdom.

The childlike Spirit

Once the disciples were arguing about which of them would be greatest in the Kingdom of heaven when it came. Jesus did not rebuke them directly, but he took a little child and set him in the midst of them; and then he said, "Truly, I say to you, unless you turn and become like children, you will never enter the Kingdom of heaven" (Matt. 18:1-4). On another occasion, when Jesus was on his last journey to Jerusalem, they brought little children to him that he should touch and bless them. The disciples were not ungracious men, but they knew that Jesus was taking his life in his hands by going to Jerusalem and they knew how tired and strained he was and what an effort it was for him to go forward; so they did not want him to be worried and bothered with the children, so they would not let the children come to him. Then Jesus said, "Let the children come to me, do not hinder them; for to such belongs the Kingdom of God" (Mark 10:13-16). It will be noted that in one of these quotations the phrase used is *the Kingdom of God*, and in the other *the Kingdom of heaven*. There is no difference whatever between the two phrases. The Jew did not readily take the name of God on his lips; if he could, he avoided it by some periphrasis. And one of the commonest ways of avoiding the name of God was to speak of heaven instead. Matthew is the most Jewish of the gospels. Matthew uses the phrase the *Kingdom of heaven* about thirty times and the *Kingdom of God* only three times. Mark and Luke speak of the *Kingdom of God* sixteen and thirty-two times respectively and do not use the phrase the *Kingdom of heaven* at all. The *Kingdom of heaven* occurs so often in Matthew simply because Matthew is so strongly Jewish and avoids taking the sacred name upon his lips as much as he can.

So then, one of the great passports to the Kingdom of God is the childlike spirit. If we are doing and obeying the will of God we will be characterised by this childlike spirit. We must note that there is a world of difference between being *childish* and being *childlike*. To be *childish* is something which deserves no praise and something out of which we should have grown long ago; but to be *childlike* is one of the greatest things in the world and one of the supreme marks of the citizens of the Kingdom.

The Child's Humility

What, then, are the qualities of the childlike spirit? First of all, there is the *humility of the child*. It was really that which was uppermost in Jesus' mind when he told the disciples that they must become as little children. These disciples looked on Jesus' Kingdom as a kingdom of this world and they were always arguing about who was going to have the biggest jobs and the highest places in it. On this particular day Jesus took a child and set him in the midst of them and said to them, "If you go on as you are doing and if you do not become like this little child, you will not get into the Kingdom at all." A little child is not interested in place and prestige and rank; he is not interested in getting the seat of honour at a feast or the first place at a king's court. He would not be in the least worried if he did not get a seat on the platform at some public function or if he did not get what people call "their place" on some public occasion. He just does not think of these things at all because he does not think of himself. It is only people who have a high idea of their own importance who speak and act like that; and a little child does not think himself important. Humility is always the sign of a really great man. Thomas Hardy was one of the greatest writers in this country. Any publisher would have been honoured to publish his books and poems and would have paid highly to do so. When Hardy was so famous that all the world knew his name, sometimes he used to send a poem to the newspapers for publication and he always enclosed a stamped addressed envelope for the return of his manuscript if the editor did not want it. Any editor would have paid highly to be allowed to publish anything Hardy wrote and would have counted it an honour to do so. Hardy never thought of that. He was so humble a man that he thought it quite possible that his manuscript would be returned. King George V was a very great king of Great Britain. The people loved him and on the occasion of his silver jubilee as king they demonstrated their love and affection in the most wonderful way. Wherever he went he was greeted with spontaneous outbursts which showed how much people thought of him. After it was all over he said to the Archbishop of Canterbury one day, "I am sure I cannot understand it, for, after all, I am only a very ordinary fellow." That was a beloved king speaking, but he was so humble a man that he thought of himself as just an ordinary fellow. No one likes a person who is conceited and —as we say—swelled-headed. The worst thing you can say about someone who sings or plays games or performs in any way, is to say, "He's good—but he knows it." Neither men nor God like a man who is proud of himself and of what he has done or can do. We must always keep ourselves humble; and it is not difficult to do that if we set our lives beside Jesus' life and compare ourselves with him. Humility is God's will for us and humility is a condition of entry and a passport to the Kingdom.

The Child's Wonder

Another thing that Jesus must have been thinking about was *the child's wonder*. A little child is always thrilled and never bored. Grown-ups require to spend a great deal of money on their pleasures; but a child can have a wonderful time with simple things which cost nothing at all. It is very easy to get bored with things and to lose the sense of wonder. In his autobiography a famous doctor called Halliday Sutherland tells how when he was a young man and newly qualified as a doctor, if there was an accident or if someone asked, "Is there a doctor present?" he was thrilled to the core to step forward and say that he was a doctor; but as he got older it became just a matter of routine; there was no thrill in it any longer; it left him bored. W. H. Davies, the tramp who was a great poet, tells how when he was quite old he went to see Tintern Abbey. As he looked at it he remembered how he had done the same twenty-seven years before when he was a young man. He says: "As I stood there now, twenty-seven years after, and compared that young boy's enthusiasm with my present lukewarm feelings, I was not very well satisfied with myself. For instance, at that time I would sacrifice both food and sleep in my travels to see anything wonderful; but now in my prime I did not go seeking things of beauty and only sang of things that came my way by chance. Judging by that wonderful feeling in boyhood I felt sure that I was only a shadow of what I should have been." At one time he had been filled with wonder; now he was only bored. We must never lose the sense of wonder and our interest in life. Many people have seen a kettle lid lifted by the steam when the water boiled, but only James Watt wondered why, and because he wondered he was able to invent the steam engine. Many people have seen an apple fall off the bough in an orchard, but only Newton wondered and so he was able to discover the law of gravity. As we get older it is dreadfully easy to lose the thrill and the wonder and the interest in life; but if we are going to live well we must keep them alive. Jesus had this sense of wonder. He said, "Consider the lilies of the field, how they grow; they neither toil nor spin; yet I tell you, even Solomon in all his glory was not arrayed like one of these" (Matt. 6:28, 29). The lilies were the little scarlet anemones that covered the hillsides in Palestine and that bloomed one day and then died; and Jesus said that even a king was not clothed like them. He wondered even at the simple things. There is one way to keep wonder alive. Think sometimes of what the world would be like *without things*—without the blue of the sky, the green of the grass, the colours of the flowers, without eyes to see them, without feet to walk and run, without a memory to remember. When we think what life would be like without God's gifts it will make us wonder at them. We must never get used to life, to the world, to our work and to our job. We must keep wonder awake for wonder also is a condition of entry and a passport to the Kingdom.

The Trust of the Child

Still further, Jesus was thinking of *the trust of the child*. Think what happens when we are very young. It is holiday time. The trunks and the cases are packed and we go to the railway or the bus station. We have no idea what train or what bus to take; we have no money to pay the fare; we would never know the way to get to our destination by ourselves. But are we worried? Not in the least, because we know that our parents will provide everything and do everything to get us to our journey's end. When we go out to the school in the morning we never doubt that when we come back the house will be there and the door open and the fire on and a meal ready. We never doubt that there will always be clothes to wear and food to eat. Why? Because we trust our parents to provide all these things for us. Suppose we were caught in a fire and could not get downstairs; suppose we were standing at a window; suppose it was quite dark and we could not see the ground. If a voice said to us. "Come on! Jump!" and we recognised that voice as our father's voice, we would not hesitate although we could not see; we know our father would not let us down. That is the way we ought to feel about God. Just as we trust our parents so we should trust God. We should always be quite sure that God will guide us and direct us and order life for us in the way that is best for us. We must always trust God for trust is the greatest of all the conditions of entry and passports to the Kingdom.

Of Such is the Kingdom of Heaven

Jesus said that the childlike spirit was a passport to the Kingdom. The humility of the child; the wonder of the child; the trust of the child are qualities we must always keep all our lives. That is God's will about how we should live. These are the passports to the Kingdom of God.

QUESTIONS FOR DISCUSSION

1. What is the difference between being childlike and childish?

2. How can we avoid becoming bored and fed up with life?

3. How can we combine humility with the strength of will and purpose which refuses to be moved from what it believes to be the right course?

6. THE FORGIVING SPIRIT

The forgiving Spirit

When we are studying the passports to the Kingdom of heaven and the conditions of citizenship of that Kingdom there is one that we meet again and again in every part of the New Testament. It is the forgiving spirit. "Blessed are the merciful" said Jesus, "for they shall obtain mercy" (Matt. 5:7). "If you do not forgive men their trespasses," Jesus warned us, "neither will your Father forgive your trespasses" (Matt. 6:15). He told a story about a man who was forgiven a colossal and unpayable debt, a debt of no less than £2,400,000, and who then went out and flung into prison a man who owed him less than £5. Jesus said that when the master who had remitted the great debt found out about this he threw the man into prison until he had paid the uttermost farthing. And then Jesus ended the story by saying, "So also my heavenly Father will do to every one of you, if you do not forgive your brother from your heart" (Matt. 18:23-35). "Judgment is without mercy," James said, "to one who has shown no mercy" (James 2:13). "Be kind to one another," said Paul, "tenderhearted, forgiving one another, even as God for Christ's sake forgave you" (Eph. 4:32). In the pages of the New Testament it is written everywhere that the forgiving spirit is a necessary passport to the Kingdom of heaven. Remember that we saw that the Kingdom of heaven is a state of things when God's will will be done as perfectly on earth as it is in heaven. Therefore, we can and must put it this way—it is God's will and God's commandment that we should forgive.

The Example of Forgiveness

We do not lack for examples of forgiveness. Think of the agony of being nailed to a cross, of having nails driven through your hands. When that was being done to him, Jesus said, "Father, forgive them; for they know not what they do" (Luke 23:34). Think of the agony of being stoned to death. When Stephen was being stoned to death, as he was dying he prayed, "Lord, do not hold this sin against them" (Acts 7:60). When George Wishart, the great Scottish reformer, was led out to be executed in St. Andrews, even the executioner hesitated to carry out the sentence. Wishart called him over to him. He kissed him on the cheek and said, "Lo, here is a token that I forgive thee; do thine office." Bryan Green, the great evangelist, tells of a mission that he carried out in America. At the end of it, anyone who wished was given just one or two minutes to give testimony of what Christ in that mission had done for him or her. A negro girl rose. She was no speaker. She could only say a few words, and she said, "Through this mission I met Jesus Christ—and he made me able to forgive the man who murdered my father." We have examples in all ages of how Jesus can enable us to forgive. This is a condition of entry to the Kingdom which life gives us the opportunity to satisfy almost every day. Let us see, then, the things we must aim at if we are to learn to forgive.

Learning to Understand

If we are to forgive *we must learn to understand*. There is a proverb which says: "To know all is to forgive all." And often if we only understand why people do things we will be able to forgive them far more easily and readily. There is always a reason why a person acts as he or she does act; and if we knew that reason we might think very differently of them. If we found a person gruff and impatient, discourteous and irritable and impolite, we might very well find that he was worried about something or perhaps that he was suffering from some pain that we knew nothing about. If we find him, as we think, mean and ungenerous and close we may find that there were reasons why he had to be. Once in a village there was a doctor. He was a good doctor and the people admired him, but he was gruff and had the name of being very close-fisted. He lived in a little village in the Highlands of Scotland; he died. On the day of the funeral the train from the south came in and out of it stepped more than a dozen men to attend the funeral. They were all doctors; some of them were specialists and some of them were even professors. And they were all men who had been poor boys and whose university fees and living expenses the old doctor had paid and had said nothing whatever about. Now the village knew why the doctor had sometimes seemed mean. And now how easy it was to forgive! If we knew the reasons why people act as they do we would understand and often we would forgive.

Take an example from industry. Not so long ago the coal-miners were accused of holding the country to ransom by their demands for higher pay and their methods of enforcing these demands. Let us always remember that less than forty years ago the average age at which miners died was thirty-eight. A hundred years ago a miner had to wear an iron collar with his owner's name engraved on it and he was legally forbidden to move beyond the area where he lived. Once I met a Welshman in Edinburgh after a rugby football international match. I got into conversation with him and this is what he said: "My grandfather was a miner, my father was a miner and I began as a miner. But I was lucky—I got my back broken in three places and I got out of the mines." He actually considered an accident like that lucky because it got him out of the mines. When we remember things like that we will not be so eager to condemn the miners for their demands. We will forgive because we will understand. Never condemn a man without at least trying to understand why he acted as he did. Far more often than not when we do understand it will be easier to forgive.

Learning to Forget

Further, if we are to forgive *we must learn to forget*. Our memories are queer things; they have a bad habit of forgetting the things we ought to remember and remembering the things we ought to forget. If someone does something unpleasant to us we are very apt to say, "I'll never forget what so-and-so did to me." We allow ourselves to think about it and brood about it, and so it gets worse all the time. It is one of the greatest faculties in the world to be able to forget the things that should be forgotten. Once the famous Scottish man of letters, Andrew Lang, wrote a very kind criticism of a new book by a certain young man. The young man, instead of being grateful, repaid Andrew Lang by a bitter and insulting attack. About three years later Andrew Lang was visiting Robert Bridges, who was then Poet Laureate. Bridges saw Lang reading a certain book; he looked at the book and saw what it was, and he said to Lang, "Why, that is a book by that ungrateful young cub who behaved so badly to you." To his astonishment he found that Andrew Lang's mind was a blank on the whole affair. He had quite forgotten the insulting attack. To forgive, said Bridges, was the sign of a great man, but to forget was sublime. We must never say that we will never forget what someone has done to us; we must never allow our minds to think and brood about anything that has been done to us. It is difficult— only Jesus can make us able to do it, but we must learn to forget.

Learning to Love

If we are to forgive, *we must learn to love others*. That is what Jesus told us to do when he told us to love our enemies (Matt. 5:44). The word Jesus uses, *to love*, is a very interesting word. It is not the same word in Greek as would be used for loving one's own family and one's nearest and dearest. It would neither be right nor possible to love our enemies as we love them. It is a word which means that no matter what the other person does to us we will never seek anything but his good. We will never do to him as he did to us; we will do to him as we would like him to do to us. Even from the point of view of

common-sense wisdom, love is better than hate. Bitterness only
begets bitterness and hatred only produces more hatred and
revenge brings still more revenge. But love is different. Once
Abraham Lincoln was blamed for being far too kind and
courteous to those who were his opponents and his enemies.
His friends told him that he was foolish to behave like that; that
his duty was to destroy his enemies. His answer was, "Do I not
destroy my enemies when I make them my friends?" When we
learn to love others then we win the greatest of all victories;
we forgive them; and by loving them, by seeking nothing but
their good, we change our enemies into our friends.

Too much Self

We have only to think about all these things to see what a
lovely thing forgiveness is. Why, then, do we find it so difficult?
Why are we so slow to forgive? One reason is that *we think far
too much about ourselves. We* have been hurt; *we* have been
injured; and that is all that we can think about. All that matters
is that something hurting and unpleasant has happened to us.
If we could get ourselves out of the picture it would make a very
great difference. It is very difficult, but we must learn to say,
"It doesn't really matter what happens to me; I'm not really
the most important person in the world; my feelings are not the
one thing that has got to be considered." When men sinned
against God, God did not think only of himself and of how
he could vindicate his honour and bring men to heel. God
thought of us and God's one thought was, "How can I win men
back to me?" That is why Jesus came to this earth, not to take
vengeance on men but to persuade them and to make it possible
for them to come back to God. We must be like God and think
not of ourselves.

Too much Pride

There is another thing which keeps us from forgiving as we
ought. *There is in us too much pride.* In our heart of hearts we
too often really think that it is a sign of weakness to forgive.
People often encourage us in that attitude. They say to us,

"You're a fool if you let so-and-so get away with that," and so because we are too proud to forgive we take the world's way and forget God's way. There was a very great Roman Emperor whose name was Marcus Aurelius. He was not only a great Emperor, he was also a great philosopher. He was not a Christian, but he was one of the finest pagans who ever lived. In a book called his *Meditations* he tells us that when he got up in the morning he would say to himself, "Today I am going to meet all kinds of unpleasant people and they are going to do all kinds of unpleasant things to me. Let me remember that it is because they do not know any better. They do not know that God is our Father and that all men are brothers; but I know; and whatever they do to me I am not going to come down to their level and I am not going to allow myself to hate them and to take vengeance on them because I know better and I must never forget the most excellent law which God has shown me." We should be like that. To forgive is not a sign of weakness; it is a sign of strength. Anyone can hate and feel bitter and try to get his own back. It takes a big man to conquer himself and to take the high way Jesus showed us. To take revenge is to copy the way of men; to forgive is to copy the way of God.

The forgiving Spirit

All over the New Testament it is made clear to us that the forgiving spirit is a necessary passport to the Kingdom of heaven and a necessary condition of citizenship of the Kingdom. If we are to forgive we must learn to understand; we must learn to forget; and we must learn to love. We must always keep ourselves out of the centre of the picture and we must remember that to forgive is a sign, not of weakness, but of strength, because to forgive is to refuse to be like others in order to be like God.

QUESTIONS FOR DISCUSSION

1. Does Christian love mean that there is no place for discipline and for punishment?

2. What would you say to someone who said: "I'll never forgive so-and-so for what he did to me"?

3. Does forgiveness mean that a wrong-doer is to escape entirely the consequences of his wrong-doing?

7. THE SERVING SPIRIT

The Spirit of Service

Jesus made it clear that very high among the conditions of citizenship of his Kingdom stands the spirit whose one desire is to serve. That becomes clear in an incident concerning James and John (Matt. 20:20-28; Mark 10:35-45). It may be that James and John wanted to get in before the others as it were. It may be that they were a little better off than the others for their father possessed hired servants to help with the work of the fishing (Mark 1:20). It may be, as Matthew seems to think, that their mother was ambitious for her sons. However that may be, they came to Jesus one day with a request. "Lord," they said, "when you come into your Kingdom, will you give us the honour of sitting one on your right hand and one on your left?" That is to say, they were trying to annex to themselves the office of chief ministers of state in Jesus' Kingdom. Jesus told them very gently that things like that were not his to give and that only if they came through the same bitter experiences as he came through could they some day share his glory. James and John accepted this; but, not unnaturally, the other disciples were very angry with them. They no doubt thought that James and John had taken a quite unfair advantage and had stolen a march upon them; and no doubt each one of them had visions of himself in the chief position in the Kingdom. Jesus knew what was going on in their minds and called them to him. He told them that they had the wrong idea altogether. "In earthly kingdoms," he said, "the greatest man is the man who exercises the greatest authority and who has the greatest power over others; but in my Kingdom," he went on, "the greatest man is the man who is the servant of all." It is not in power but in service that greatness in that Kingdom counts.

The Great Servants

So, then, the desire to serve is a passport to the Kingdom. Jesus said, "Whoever would save his life will lose it; and whoever loses his life for my sake, he will save it" (Luke 9:24). Jesus meant that if we hug and hoard life to ourselves then we only succeed in losing what really makes life worth living; whereas if we generously and even recklessly spend life for others, we gain everything that makes life worth while. Cosmo Lang, who became Archbishop of Canterbury, had once aimed at a great secular career. A godly friend's influence made him abandon his ambitions and enter the ministry of the Church of England. When he was studying for the ministry at Cuddesdon he was in the Chapel praying one day, and as he prayed, he heard unmistakably a voice saying to him, "You are wanted!" He knew that God needed him not for worldly ambition but for service. There was a preacher and evangelist called Christmas Evans. He was continually on the road preaching and working for Christ. His friends used to urge him to take it easier and to husband his strength. His answer was, "It is better to burn out than to rust out." When Joan of Arc knew that her time was bound to be short and that her enemies were sure to destroy her very soon, she prayed to God, "I shall only last a year; use me as you can." She did not pray to be spared and preserved; she prayed to be used, for her one desire was to serve. Frances Ridley Havergal wrote in her hymn:

> "O use me, Lord, use even me,
>> Just as thou wilt, and when, and where,
> Until Thy blessed face I see,
>> Thy rest, Thy joy, Thy glory share."

It is the same prayer, the prayer not to be spared but to be used in service. In this life there are two kinds of people. There are the people who take out of life more than they put in; and there are the people who put into life more than they take out. There are the people whose aim is to do the minimum permissible; and there are the people whose aim it is to do the maximum possible. The people who are citizens of the Kingdom are those whose one desire is to be used; to spend life generously; always to give far more than they get.

Witnessing for God

How, then, can we begin on this life of service? How can we serve God? We can serve God *by being his witnesses wherever we are and wherever we go*. Instead of *witnesses*, let us use another word which will make this more real to us; we can serve God by always being good *advertisements* for the Christian way. A witness for God is someone who is never ashamed in any circumstances to show whose he is and whom he is seeking to serve. Inevitably people watch us, and whether we like it or not we are good or bad advertisements for Christianity. By the way in which we live we either make people think that Christianity must be a splendid thing; or we make them think that a faith that produces people like us cannot be much good. The way in which a person professing to be a Christian behaves can make all the difference in the world. Randolph Sturgess became a great figure in the life of the Salvation Army. When he was young he was a Church worker. His job was to blow the bellows of the organ while the organist played; and it was hard work, but he was happy to do it for the sake of the Church. A Prayer Meeting was started before the services in a little room in the Church. Randolph attended it because he wanted to learn more about God. One evening at this meeting something really happened and he gave his heart to God. He was thrilled by this experience and with all his new happiness in his heart he went to the organ loft to do his usual job. He was just a little late because that night the meeting for prayer had lasted a little longer. The organist was walking up and down in a fury. When, however, Randolph appeared, he burst out at him in a blazing temper. He actually swore at him for being a few minutes late and never asked why he was late. Randolph said to himself, "Is that the way that Christians can speak?" His new-found joy was spoiled by the conduct of a man who was a very bad advertisement for the faith he was supposed to serve. By being courteous, kind, unselfish, honourable, happy and true, we can serve God by showing others what a splendid thing the Christian life can be.

Serving God by serving Others

Further, we can serve God *by serving others*. Jesus said, "As you did it to one of the least of these my brethren, you did it to me" (Matt. 25:40). One of the best ways of serving God's kingdom is to serve God's men. A certain Mrs. Berwick who had once worked in social work for the Salvation Army in Liverpool, retired from active work and in her old age came to stay in London. The war came with the terrible air raids. People used to get queer ideas in those dangerous days and they got the idea that her poor house and her Anderson shelter were specially safe. She was old now, but she felt that she must do something about this. Her Liverpool days lay far distant, but her instinct to bind up wounds and alleviate suffering made her assemble a first-aid box and place in her window a notice: "If you need help, knock here." That is what every member of the Kingdom must be like. We should be far more concerned about other people than we are about ourselves. Once a schoolboy was asked what parts of speech *my* and *mine* were. He answered that they were *aggressive pronouns*! This world is full of aggressive people whose favourite words are *I* and *me* and *my* and *mine*. These people are citizens of the world and no doubt they do well enough in the world; but the citizen of the Kingdom thinks not of himself but of others. If we keep thinking about what we can get and about what we can succeed in making others do for us we are far away from the Kingdom; but if all the time we keep thinking of what we can give and of what we can do for others then we, too, are within the Kingdom.

Service in Work

But the greatest of all ways of serving is *at our daily work*. There are three ways of doing our work. (a) We can do our work thinking only about what we are going to get out of it.

We can do it simply and solely for pay. To tell the truth, that is what most people do. Of course, it is an honourable thing to work for a week's wage; but to think of nothing but the wage is wrong. General George Carpenter, of the Salvation Army, tells how in Buenos Aires a man became a follower of Christ. He was doing what so many of the Salvationists do, he was selling the Army's newspaper, *The War Cry*. He offered copies to two business men in a café. They immediately asked him, "What do you get out of selling these papers?" He said he got nothing; that he did it simply for the love of the work. They simply would not believe it, until he had actually taken steps to prove it to them. They were so astonished at any man getting nothing out of his work that they invited him to come to their homes to tell them why he did this. He went and told them and at the end of the story, they, too, became Christians. You see how two businessmen were astonished that any man should not first ask, "What do I get out of this?" Simply to work for pay is a mark of the world's way and is the opposite of the ways of the Kingdom. (b) We may work from a sense of duty. That is much better. To take another story from the Salvation Army: Mrs. General Carpenter tells us how, as a girl, she hated duty. She says, "My mother was a perfect housekeeper. In bedmaking this perfection involved putting on the sheets in such a way that one turned down the top sheet with the hem inside. 'The fag! The nonsense!' I said to myself. . . . That morning, clear as a bell, I heard the still, small Voice say, 'If you don't take yourself in hand and make yourself do things properly, you will be of no use in my Kingdom.' Then I pulled the bed to pieces and, for the first time in my life, made it properly without hating the job." There is one thing quite certain—God cannot use a person who shirks his duty. We must always faithfully do our work as a duty. But that is still not enough. The very word *duty* has a hard sound; duty may be something that is done grimly and unwillingly although conscientiously. We must go further yet. (c) We may work *for God*. And we really become God's servants, we really acquire the spirit of service, we really become citizens of the Kingdom when we work for God.

A. J. Cronin, the famous author, tells of a district nurse he met when he was a doctor. "For nearly twenty years she had worked single-handed in a certain district, a ten-mile round, a never-ending day. I marvelled at her fortitude, her patience and her cheerfulness. She was never too tired at night to rise for an urgent call. Her salary was most inadequate, and late one night, after a particularly strenuous day, I ventured to protest to her. 'Nurse, why don't you make them pay you more? God knows you are worth it.' 'If God knows I'm worth it,' she said, 'that's all that matters to me.' In a flash I saw the rich significance of her life and the comparative emptiness of my own." Here was a lady whom everyone loved and who served her people ungrudgingly and unfailingly because she was working for God. She did not care what verdict men passed on her work; she cared only for God's verdict. She did not care for men's pay; she cared only for God's "Well done!" Every time we do a thing we should ask, "How would God like me to do it?" When we have done a thing we should ask, "Can I take this and show it to God?" If we do that we will be filled with this spirit of service because we will know that we can never do enough to do well enough for God. We must never think of God as being only in the Church or the Bible Class, or as being present only on Sundays. If all day, every day, we feel God's presence then we are bound to be filled with the spirit of service because we will always be trying to do the things which will make him glad to see.

The serving Spirit

Jesus made it quite clear to James and John that greatness in his Kingdom consisted not of power but of service, not of controlling others but of serving them. The really great people have felt God calling on them to serve and have been compelled to answer the call. We can serve God by witnessing for him everywhere; by serving the men and women who are his sons and daughters; by doing all our work, not for pay, not even for duty, but for himself. Then we will be obeying his will all the time and then we will be citizens of the Kingdom.

1. Is it possible to be a really Christian workman under present day industrial conditions?

2. What is the difference between right and wrong ambition?

3. How ought we to live to witness for Christ?

8. THE WORTH OF THE KINGDOM

The Supreme Value of the Kingdom

To Jesus the Kingdom of God was the most precious thing in all the universe and citizenship of it was of all things most valuable. Repeatedly He made it clear that the Kingdom had a value and a worth which were above all earthly things and standards. He said, "Seek first the Kingdom of God" (Matt. 6:33). He said, "If your eye causes you to sin, pluck it out; it is better for you to enter the Kingdom of God with one eye than with two eyes to be thrown into hell (Mark 9:43-48; cf. Matt. 5:29, 30; 18:8). He put it in another way when he said, "What will it profit a man, if he gains the whole world and forfeits his life?" (Matt. 16:25). He told two stories (Matt. 13:44-46) about the value of the Kingdom. He said that once there was a man who was digging in a field; as he dug his spade struck across a buried treasure. It was the Jewish law that such finds might be retained by the finder; and so the man went away and sold every single thing that he possessed in order that he might buy the field and so possess the treasure. He said that once there was a merchant man who had spent his whole life searching for lovely pearls. At last he found a pearl which was the loveliest pearl he had ever seen; so, when he had found it, he went and sold up his whole stock and everything he had in order to buy the one precious pearl. It is that way, said Jesus, that a man must be about the Kingdom. To become a citizen of the Kingdom is worth everything that a man possesses and everything that a man is; and if anything hinders a man from becoming a citizen of it, even if that thing is the dearest thing on earth, it must be rooted out and thrown away. Now let us remember that we may put all this in another way. Let us repeat our definition— the Kingdom of God is a society upon earth in which God's will is as perfectly done as it is in heaven. Therefore we may say that the most precious thing on earth, the thing for which all else must be sacrificed and given up, the thing which must come first in life, is the doing of God's will.

The Key to Happiness

Why, then, is citizenship of the Kingdom so supremely valuable? Why is it so precious perfectly to do God's will? For one thing, *it is the way to happiness*. Here we have a paradox. To do God's will may very well be the way to everything that the world calls trouble. It may be the way to loss and persecution, to unpopularity and isolation, even to death—and yet it remains that it is the way to happiness. Let us take the story of how two people came to the end of life. The first was Judas. He betrayed Jesus for thirty pieces of silver; he went right against God's will to win that bribe from the Jewish authorities. What happened to him? When he saw what he had done he went to the authorities and tried to undo his dreadful bargain. They only laughed at him and he went out and hanged himself (Matt. 27:3-5). He had gone against God's will. By doing so he had made money and had gained favour with the most influential people in the land; but it made him so wretchedly unhappy that he committed suicide. The other person is Jesus. In Gethsemane Jesus faced God's will; that will for him was the Cross; he prayed that there might be some other way, and when he knew that there was no other way he said, "Thy will be done." Jesus, too, died and he died in all the agony of the Cross; but he died with a cry of triumph on his lips for his last words were the victor's shout: "It is finished!" Who was the happy man? The happy one was he who did God's will and found in it the way to death but also the way to triumph. To do God's will may get us into what men call trouble, but it is the way to a happiness that nothing else can ever bring. At one time the Salvation Army people in India were persecuted and even imprisoned in the most terrible circumstances. One of them, Brother Glacken, afterwards wrote: "The few days I was in Chauki (in prison) were the happiest days of my life. It was like Paradise there, for I felt the presence of the Lord Jesus greatly." If he had dodged the will of God, if he had refused to be true and loyal to Jesus, these days would not have been spent in the terrible conditions of an Indian prison, but for all that they would have been the most wretched days of his life; but he did God's will; he was loyal and true; he did end in prison; but the days in prison were the happiest days of his life.

A Goal for Life

Wherein lies the happiness of doing God's will? For one thing, *to do God's will gives us a goal in life.* One of the unhappiest things in life is to have nothing to do; to be mooning about with no interest and with nothing special to do. We all know those days when we were at a loose end and when we said, "What will I do now?" and when we were a nuisance to ourselves and to everyone else. Life is always the same. The man who drifts through life without a goal is never really happy. It may be a terrific struggle to reach the goal, but there is a thrill even in the struggle. Everyone knows how much the Scots people value knowledge and learning; how much Scots families sacrificed and suffered to send their sons to the university. Sir James Barrie writes about these days like this: "I knew three undergraduates who lodged together in a dreary house at the top of a dreary street. Two of them used to study till two in the morning while the third slept. When they shut their books they awoke number three who arose, dressed and studied till breakfast time. Among the many advantages of this arrangement was that, as they were dreadfully poor, one bed did for the three. Two of them occupied it at one time and the third at another. Terrible privation? Dreadful destitution? Not a bit of it; if life was at the top of a hundred steps, if students occasionally died of hunger and hard work combined, if the midnight oil burned to show a ghastly face weary and worn, if lodgings were cheap and dirty and dinners few and far between, life was real and earnest and it did not turn out an empty dream." It was because they had a goal they could do this and get a thrill out of doing it. Things are easier in that line now, but there are still students who work as bus conductors, railway porters, proof readers in the great newspaper offices all night, even labourers on the roads, in order to get enough money to get knowledge. They have a goal and life is a thrill even when things are desperately hard.

Now if in everything in life we have the one aim of, by the help of Jesus, doing God's will, that gives us an object in life and, given an objective like that, life becomes quite different. Instead of going nowhere it is definitely going somewhere. Instead of being boring and wearisome it becomes adventurous and thrilling. An American traveller had to cross a ferry over a river every day. The engineer was a negro and for long the engine-room of the ferry was a dirty and untidy place. One day when the traveller got on to the ferry he noticed a change. The engine-room was spotless; even the brass piping shone until you could see your face in it. He could not help commenting on the change. He said to the engineer, "What's happened?" "Sir," said the engineer, "I've got glory." He had become a Christian and because he was a Christian there was a kind of new glory in life that made him make even the dirty engine-room of the old ferry boat a shining place. When we have this objective of doing the will of God the new glory and the new happiness come into life.

The Joy of doing the right Thing

For another thing, citizenship of the Kingdom brings happiness because it gives us *the joy of doing the right thing*. We can get a certain joy out of games and what the world calls pleasure and out of doing what we like. But it is a joy that does not last; and there is always a nagging little unhappiness at the back of it because we are always conscious that there is something which we should be doing or which we should have done. The deepest satisfaction in the world is the satisfaction of a job well and truly done. W. E. Henley, the Scots poet, wrote somes lines about how he would like life to end for him:

> "So be my passing,
>   My task accomplished and the long day done.
>   My wages taken and in my heart
>   Some late lark singing,
>   Let me be gathered to the quiet west,
>   The sundown splendid and serene."

The greatest joy is to have a task accomplished; the long day done and nothing left undone. If we then devote ourselves always to doing the will of God we will always have that joy of having done the right thing and we will be citizens of the Kingdom.

Useful to Others

But there is more than that—*citizenship of the Kingdom makes us useful to others*. The value of it lies not only in our own happiness; if that were all, it would be a seifish thing. It lies in the fact that, when a man seeks ever to do the will of God and not his own will, he becomes a useful citizen of the community. When a man becomes obedient to God of necessity he becomes of double use to his fellow men. Suppose a man is a drunkard. He is a nuisance to himself; he is a tragedy for those with whom he lives; he is a danger to the community. Then suppose this man takes Jesus as his Master and his Lord and seeks to become a citizen of the Kingdom by doing God's will. The immediate result is that the man who was once a bad debt to the community becomes a useful member of the community. Now, so long as we are living life in obedience to our own wishes and not in obedience to the will of God, what is the characteristic of our lives? We can sum it up in one word—*selfishness*. So long as we are selfish we think only of ourselves; we do not even think of being of use to others. We have already seen that the spirit of service is one of the great passports to the Kingdom. Therefore when we become citizens of the Kingdom, when we begin to try to do God's will we cease to be selfish and we become filled with the desire to be of use to all. The great worth of the Kingdom lies in the fact that it brings us happiness and it makes us useful to others.

The Kingdom and the Life to come

Citizenship of the Kingdom looks beyond this life. When this life comes to an end, when we die, life is not finished. There is a life to come. And the kind of life we have lived here will make all the difference to the kind of life we will live in the world to come. In school we cannot move up to a higher class until we have faithfully done the work of a lower class. Unless we had faithfully done the tasks of the lower class we would not be fit for the higher tasks of the higher class. Life is like that. To die is like moving up to a higher class. Think of it this way. When we are choosing what we are going to be, someone may say to us, "Now, you must choose very carefully, because you are going to spend your life in that job and you must be careful in the choice of something in which you are going to spend your life." But in the world to come we are not only going to spend a lifetime; we are going to spend an eternity; and if that be so, surely we should be very careful how we prepare ourselves for it. In that world to come we will be very directly in God's presence. That must mean that we can be happy there only if we have done God's will. And so to do God's will is not only the thing which brings us happiness in this life; it brings us happiness also in the life to come. That is why it is so important to become a citizen of the Kingdom. It is worth much to be happy in this life; it is worth still more to be useful to others; but it is worth most of all to find happiness in the life to come which is to last for ever. And we can only find these things when our will is God's will and God's will is our will; that is, when we are really and truly citizens of his Kingdom.

The Worth of the Kingdom

To be in the Kingdom means to do God's will. And that is the most precious and valuable and important thing in the world because it makes us happy; it makes us useful; and it will some day make heaven for us a place of joy.

QUESTIONS FOR DISCUSSION

1. If doing God's will makes us useful, what would you say about those who withdraw from life to live in a monastery or a convent?

2. Do you think that a person can be a Christian without believing in a life to come?

3. If doing God's will means serving people and making life better for others, should a Christian therefore be active in politics, in local government, in trade unions, in social service?

9. THE NECESSITY OF DECISION

The Necessity of Decision

The whole Bible makes it quite clear that to become a citizen of the Kingdom is a matter which requires a definite decision. No one ever drifted into the Kingdom and no one ever became a citizen of the Kingdom, as it were, by accident and unawares. If we are to become citizens of the Kingdom we must of necessity make up our minds about it and decide what we are going to do. It might be said that the whole Bible is one long sermon on the word *Choose*. Away back in the very early days, towards the end of his life, Moses assembled the people and said to them, "I call heaven and earth to witness against you this day, that I have set before you life and death, blessing and curse; therefore *choose* life" (Deut. 30:19). Again, when Joshua's life work had come to an end he put before the people the definite choice, "*Choose* this day whom you will serve" (Josh. 24:15). There is in the Old Testament one vivid picture of what happened to a woman who could not make up her mind. In Genesis there is the strange old story of Lot's wife. The cities of the plain, Sodom and Gomorrah, had lived so wickedly that they were to be destroyed. Lot and his family were warned to leave them before the destruction fell upon them. So they went out and then there comes the sentence:

"But Lot's wife behind him looked back, and she became a pillar of salt" (Gen. 19:26). It is the picture of a woman who could not make up her mind; she knew she must not stay in the cities but she had a lingering desire to go back; she could not come to a clear-cut decision and disaster overtook her. And Jesus himself, as Luke tells us, once said to his followers, "Remember what happened to Lot's wife" (Luke 17:32). There was one incident in Jesus' life which showed how important he believed it to be that a man should make up his mind. A man came to him and said he desired to follow him, but first he wanted to go home and to say goodbye to the people at home. Jesus said, "No one who puts his hand to the plough and looks back is fit for the Kingdom of God" (Luke 9:61, 62). The whole Bible makes it quite clear that to become a citizen of the Kingdom is a matter of deliberate choice; it is something about which it is utterly essential that we should make up our minds.

The Dislike of Decision

People very commonly dislike having to decide. Many of us, if not most of us, put off making decisions as long as we possibly can. And that is a mistake. In one of the Christopher Robin poems there are these lines:

> "Halfway down the stairs
> Is a stair
> Where I sit.
> There isn't
> Any other stair
> Quite like it.
> I'm not at the bottom,
> I'm not at the top;
> So this is the stair
> Where I always stop.
> Halfway up the stairs
> Isn't up
> And isn't down.
> It isn't in the nursery,
> It isn't in the town

And all sorts of funny thoughts
Run round my head.
It isn't really anywhere,
It's somewhere else instead."

The person who will not come to a decision is like the person halfway upstairs. He is neither up nor down. He is not really anywhere. John Oxenham wrote the famous lines:

"To every man there openeth
A way, and ways, and a way,
The high soul climbs the high way,
The low soul gropes the low,
And in between, on the misty flats
The rest drift to and fro.
But to every man there openeth
A high way, and a low.
And every man decideth
The way his soul shall go."

There he talks about the unhappy people who drift to and fro undecidedly. Life must always be a failure until we decide definitely what we are going to do. And very specially, to become a citizen of the Kingdom requires an act of decision on our part.

The Destruction of Effectiveness

Indecision is always a fatal thing. For one thing, *indecision destroys effectiveness*. We can never really be effective until we make up our minds and until we stop—to use the common word—dithering. In the early days in Greece there was a school of philosophers called the Sceptics. Their basic belief was that no one could ever be sure of anything and that therefore a man must never make up his mind about anything. They used all kinds of queer arguments. They said, "There's a stick. What kind of stick is it?" You would answer, "It looks quite straight." They then put the stick half in and half out of water and said "How does the straight stick look now?" And, of course, the answer was, "It looks bent!" They said, "How do you know a thing is sweet? The same thing will taste sweet after you have sipped vinegar and sour after you have tasted honey!" So the

Sceptics said, "You can't be sure of anything; you can't say anything is certain." Therefore they said, "The wise man must never decide"; he must always remain in a state of suspended judgment. The only result of this was that no Sceptic ever did anything worth while, because action was paralysed because he would not decide.

Before we can act we must decide. Sometimes at games we see a player get the ball. He obviously does not know what he is going to do with it. The only result is that he loses it, or falls over it; and the crowd roars at him, "Make up your mind!" If we are going to be effective in life we must make up our minds and, above all, if we are going to be citizens of the Kingdom we must decide for Jesus.

The Destruction of Happiness

Further, *indecision destroys happiness*. No one can be happy so long as he is drawn in two directions at once. Beverley Nichols tells in his autobiography about an interview he had with Queen Sophie of Greece in which she told him of her heartbreaking position in the 1914-18 war when England was at war with Germany. She had very close ties with both countries. She said, "I loved England; I was brought up there. I had dozens of relations there and literally hundreds of friends. But," she went on, "I loved Germany too, and the German Emperor was my brother. So torn between the two countries I lived in a horrible No Man's Land of indecision." It is always an unhappy thing to be undecided. We talk about being *distracted*; the English word comes from the Latin word *distrahere* which literally means to drag a person or thing apart. No one can be happy if he is the centre of a kind of mental tug-of-war. If we are going to have any peace in life we must make up our minds one way or another; and, above all, whether or not we are going to become members of the Kingdom and whether or not we are going to decide for Jesus.

The Destruction of Loyalty

Still further, *indecision is the destruction of loyalty*. As we have already seen Jesus said, "No one can serve two masters"

(Matt. 6:24). We cannot be in love with two people at the same time. We must take the decision to be wholeheartedly loyal to the one or to the other. One of the great disasters in shipping was when the new liner *Titanic*, on her maiden voyage, struck a submerged iceberg and sank with tragic loss of life. On board her were Ernest and Lilian Carter. They were husband and wife; for fourteen years they had served the poor people in Whitechapel and they were taking a holiday for the first time in all these years. The ship struck and was sinking fast. They were standing together on the deck after all the boats were filled. Suddenly a voice came from one of the boats, "Come on, Mrs. Carter, there's room for you here." For answer she linked her arm through her husband's, and they heard her say, "I'm staying with you." She made her decision. There was only one love in her life. It is specially that way with Jesus. No one can really be half a Christian and half not. Someone put it this way: "There is no place for neutrality in the Christian life." We have got to be out and out for Jesus or we cannot serve him at all. To be a citizen of the Kingdom needs an act of decision; we must decide whether or not we are for Jesus.

The Decision which can be refused

Now this is a decision which can be refused. There is a story in the New Testament of a man who refused the decision. We call him the Rich Young Ruler. He came hurrying down the street and knelt at Jesus' feet and said, "What must I do to inherit eternal life?" (That is just another way of saying, "How can I become a citizen of the Kingdom?") Jesus told him to keep the commandments. He said he had done so all his life. Jesus could see into the heart of this young man and he knew that the one thing he really cared for was money, ease and comfort; that he was really living a selfish life; that he had everything and gave nothing away; that his possessions had far too big a grip of him. So Jesus said to him, "If you really want to be perfect, sell all that you have got and give it to the poor; and you will be rich in heaven." And the young man would not do it. And then there is one last sentence: he went away grieved. He knew quite well what decision he ought to have taken; and he knew he had not taken it; that is why he went away grieved. It is quite possible to refuse to take the decision to become a citizen of the Kingdom; but a refusal like that can only end in sorrow (Mark 10:17:22).

A Citizen of the Kingdom

When we take this decision what are we deciding to do? We are deciding that we will take Jesus as our Master and our Lord and that we will be loyal to him no matter what the cost. Let us put it another way. We decide that we will take God's will and we will obey that will every day and all the time. That will be a very difficult decision to take and it will be a still more difficult decision to keep. It will specially require one thing. It will require that we should keep constant touch with Jesus. It means that we will always have to be asking him, "What do you want me to do?" and it means that we will always have to be asking him for strength to do it. When C. T. Studd, the famous cricketer, felt he had received a call to be a missionary in China it made his mother very sad. Studd said, "Let us ask God about it. I don't want to be pig-headed and go out there of my own accord. I just want to do God's will. So," he goes on, "we went down on our knees and put the whole matter in God's hands. That night I could not get to sleep, but it seemed as though I heard someone say these words over and over, 'Ask of me and I will give you the heaven for thine inheritance and the uttermost parts of the earth for thy possession.' " And Studd knew he had to go. In his problem he asked God and God gave him guidance and strength. A Salvation Army officer heard a girl pray: "My Dear God, if you expect me to keep my temper with Mr. Jones and to be patient with Mabel, you will have to give me a spot of help!" The girl put it just in her own way, but if we decide to be citizens of the Kingdom, and if we ask God what he wants us to do and for strength to do it, we can be quite sure that we will never lack his guidance and his help.

The Necessity of Decision

Whether or not to become a citizen of the Kingdom is something we must decide for ourselves. Most people do not like making decisions, but indecision destroys effectiveness; it destroys happiness; and it destroys loyalty. We must make up our minds however difficult it is; and if we ask him, God will always tell us what he wants us to do and will always give us strength to do it.

QUESTIONS FOR DISCUSSION

1. What exactly does it mean to decide for Christ?
2. Could you decide for Christ and have nothing to do with the Church?
3. How will the life of the person who has decided for Christ differ from the life of the person who has not decided for Christ?

10. THE NECESSITY OF EFFORT

There is nothing worth getting in this world which can be got without an effort. If we are to excel at any game we must practise long hours until we can master all its technique and overcome all its difficulties. We must train our bodies until they are fit and strong enough to answer to its strenuous activity. If we are to excel at any art we must study and practise, perhaps for years, perhaps even for a lifetime. If we are to do well at work we must be prepared to do the extra study and the extra training which alone will take us to the top. In this world nothing which is really worth while drops into our hands; it has got to be striven for and to be paid for in the coin of toil and endeavour. When you see an expert do a thing it all looks so easy and so effortless; but that effortless ease is the result of hours of unremitting and unrelenting toil and effort. It has been said that genius is an infinite capacity for taking pains. It has been said that the characteristic of all great men was that they could toil terribly. What is true of life is true of the citizenship of the Kingdom. To be a citizen of the Kingdom is something which demands effort and which takes everything of mind and heart and body that a man can give.

The Conqueror

There are two very suggestive things in the New Testament which go to prove that. (a) The New Testament has a habit of making all its promises to the man who overcomes, to the conqueror (cp. Rev. 2:7, 11, 17, 26; 3:5, 12, 21). To become a citizen of the Kingdom is a triumph and a conquest and no victory is ever won without blood and sweat and tears. (b) The New Testament is full of imperatives. The man who will be a citizen of the Kingdom is a man under orders. The Sermon on the Mount contains no fewer than forty-two imperatives. It is as if Jesus was always urging men to greater and greater efforts of obedience and loyalty and achievement. We may look briefly at just two of these imperatives. Jesus said, "*Seek* first the Kingdom of God and his righteousness" (Matt. 6:33; Luke 12:31). That could well be translated, "Make the Kingdom of God the object of your whole endeavour." Bend every single particle and atom of energy you possess to attain citizenship of the Kingdom. Jesus said, "Strive to enter by the narrow door" (Luke 13:24). The verb that is used for strive comes from a Greek noun, *agōn*, which means a contest. It is the word from which there comes the English word *agony*. We may say, quite literally, that the struggle to enter into the Kingdom and to become one of its citizens is so intense that it is an agony. Jesus said, "The Kingdom of God is preached and everyone enters it violently" (Luke 16:16). The Greek word that is used for to enter violently is a strong word. It is the word that is used for storming a city and forcing an entry. It could be translated, "Everyone forces his way into it." Denney, commenting on this verse, said: "The Kingdom of heaven is not for the well-meaning but for the desperate." Everthing goes to show this tremendous effort which a man must put forth to become a member and a citizen of the Kingdom.

The Conquest of ourselves

We must ask, then, What are the things that we must conquer? First and foremost, *there are things in ourselves which we must conquer.* (a) We must conquer our natural *laziness.* The queer thing in life is that although we are often prepared to reduce ourselves to exhaustion doing things which are not of any great importance, we are very unwilling to make a big effort to do the things which are really important. We will play games or go dancing until we are ready to drop; we will spend endless time and thought and energy upon a hobby; but we will not readily make any such effort to learn lessons or to acquire the knowledge that we need. When Ulysses and his sailors came to the island where the lotus-flower grew the sailors foolishly ate of the lotus. The characteristic and the property of the lotus was that it made a man forget his home and his friends and made him want to lie and laze in that land "where it was always afternoon". We must conquer that laziness which keeps us from making an effort in the really worthwhile things. (b) We must conquer our *temper*. Alexander the Great was the conqueror of the world, the man who wept because there were no more worlds left to conquer. But once at a feast, when he had taken too much wine, he lifted his spear and hurled it through his best friend and killed him. The man who had conquered the world could not conquer himself and so brought his best friend death and himself sorrow. The man who is going to be the servant of others must first master himself. The lad with the uncontrolled temper is a bad debt to his team and his side and his friends. (c) We must conquer our desire to take the easy way. It is almost instinct to try to avoid trouble. Once when the statues in an old cathedral were being examined, it was discovered that in one part the front of the statues was perfectly carved; every detail was exact; but the back where no one could see was left rough and unfinished and incomplete. But in another cathedral when the roof was being cleaned, there was found a carving perfect in every detail in a place where no one would ever see it. These two things stand for two kinds of workmen—the workman who cannot be bothered to do the thing properly if he can get away with doing it in the easy way, and the workman who will do the things to the utmost of his ability even though there be no one there to see. No real man takes the easy and the shoddy way, but we have to conquer ourselves if everything is to be the utmost for the highest all the time. (d) We have to conquer *discouragement*. Sometimes it is very hard to keep on when we do not seem to be getting any-where. Sometimes we think that we will never master a subject. Sometimes it does seem that everything is against us. When Carlyle had finished the first volume of his book, *The French Revolution*, he gave it to a friend called Mill to read and to criticise. On 6th March, 1835—he never forgot the date—Mill called on him to say that the manuscript had accidentally been burned and completely destroyed. Half a year's work was gone for nothing. Worse, the inspiration was gone because it is always hard to recapture the verve and the vigour if a man has to do a thing like that twice. But Carlyle set out to do the whole thing again, and to his wife he said a very wonderful thing. He said, "We must try to conceal from Mill the extent of the damage he has done." Many a man might have been angry and bitter, but Carlyle thought more of Mill's worry than of his own loss. Many a man would simply have given up but Carlyle refused to be discouraged and kept on. The real test of an army is how it fights when it is hungry and tired and beaten. The real test of a team is how it plays when it is two or three goals down. One of the biggest tests of any man is how he reacts to discouragement. Does he collapse under it, or does he conquer it, as a true man must?

The Conquest of Temptation

Further, one of the great victories we must win is the victory over *temptation*. It is impossible to go through this life and not to be tempted. Right at the beginning of his ministry Jesus was tempted to take the wrong way. There are two ways of overcoming temptation. (a) One of the best ways of over-coming temptation is to realise where the wrong thing leads and what it does. We have heard of a man who often allowed drink to conquer him. One day, when he was more than half drunk, he was going into a building. The building had glass swing doors. As he went in he saw his own reflection in the swing doors and saw what drink made him look like. And the sight of himself under the influence of drink cured him from drinking once and for all. He saw what it could do. Once in America a judge took a very original way of sentencing a man.

This man had been arrested for driving under the influence of drink. He was found guilty. The judge did not fine him and did not send him to prison. He ordered him to spend the next month as a permanent resident in the casualty receiving ward of a great hospital. Day in, day out, night and day for a month that man saw people, who were all victims of street accidents being brought into that ward, injured and smashed up. When that man suddenly realised what accidents can do to people he swore he would never be found under the influence of drink in charge of a motor car again. He now saw what terrible harm such foolishness could do. There is one way in which anyone can see what sin can do. We have only to look at the Cross of Jesus to see it. Jesus was the loveliest and the wisest and the best person who ever lived. No one was ever so kind; no one was ever so helpful to so many people; no one ever spoke words of such truth. And yet men took and crucified him on a cross. It was sin which did that and when we see what sin has done we must surely hate sin with an utter hatred. (b) Another way of conquering temptation is to remember *how important it is to please God and to do God's will*. If someone is very good to us we always want to show our gratitude. It sometimes happens at home that we get a really expensive present, something that we have always wanted and longed for. It usually happens that for at least a day or two after that we are as good as gold, because we feel that in view of what we have received we cannot in decency and fairness be anything else! We have only to think of what God gave us—this wonderful life, this beautiful world, and above all the gift of his Son, Jesus. That should make us feel that there is nothing in this world so supremely important as trying to please and to bring joy to God—and we can only do that by doing his will.

The Helper

So then, it will take a tremendous effort to become a citizen of the Kingdom. To become a citizen of the Kingdom requires a victory and a triumph and a conquest. No one drifts into the Kingdom; we have to struggle and to battle our way in. All this is very difficult, and the natural thing to say is that we can never do that by ourselves. Neither we can; and we are not asked to. With us all the time is the help of Jesus. Jesus never tried to hide the fact that he was sending out his men on a very difficult assignment. He told them they would be like sheep in the midst of wolves; that they would be brought before rulers and governors and councils and that they would be cross-examined and scourged and condemned; that they would be hated for his name's sake; that they must take up their own cross and follow after him (Matthew 10:16-23). But then at the very end he said to them as it were, "I know what you are going to face; but do not be afraid, for lo, I am with you always, even to the end of the world" (Matthew 28:20). If it were left to us ourselves we could never get into the Kingdom at all. But the King is with us to enable us to do the things which by ourselves we could never have done.

The Necessity of Effort

All worthwhile things demand effort and so does the Kingdom. To enter the Kingdom requires a victory. We must conquer ourselves, our natural laziness, the quickness of our temper, our way of looking for the easy way, the discouragements that life inevitably brings. We must conquer our temptations; and we can do that by realising the harm that temptation may do and by realising all that God has done for us so that our dearest wish will be to do his will. For ourselves to do this would be completely impossible, but that which is impossible for us alone becomes possible when Jesus is with us.

QUESTIONS FOR DISCUSSION

1. Why is it that we are prepared to give so much effort to a game or a hobby when we are not prepared to give the same effort to learning and studying something useful?

2. Examine yourself, and see what weaknesses you have to conquer, and see against what particular temptation you must be specially on guard.

3. Through what influences do temptations come to us?

11. THE MORAL DEMANDS OF THE KINGDOM

The Necessity of being different

The Christian is a man who is a citizen of the Kingdom of heaven. In this world citizens of different countries behave in different ways. We would not be likely to mistake a Frenchman for a German, or a German for a Frenchman or a person of our own country for either. Therefore it is quite clear that the citizen of the Kingdom of heaven must be different from people who are merely citizens of this world. The New Testament over and over again insists that the Christian must live a life worthy of his Christianity, that the citizen of the Kingdom must live according to the laws of the Kingdom. We can come at this a great many different ways. A person might say, What use is there in being a Christian? The only compelling answer to that is to show that Christianity produces a better person than any other kind of faith or life. Or a person might say, You say you are a Christian; but how am I to know that you are a Christian? The only compelling answer to that is that we can only show that we are Christians by doing Christian things.

The Demand of the New Testament

So Jesus always insisted that if Christianity had no effect upon a man's life and character, on his deeds and actions, it was not really Christianity. Even before Jesus came out into the open as a preacher and teacher, John the Baptist made the same demand. When people came to him to be baptised, he challenged them, "Bear fruit that befits repentance" (Matt. 3:8). He meant, show by your actions that you really are a changed person. When Paul was telling about the task that God had given him to do, he said to King Agrippa that he preached to the Gentiles that they should repent and that they should do works worthy of repentance (Acts 26:20). It is the same demand again, that men should prove the change in their lives by a change in their deeds. Jesus was very plain about this. He said, "You will know them by their fruits" (Matt. 7:20). You can tell what kind of a man a man is by what he does.

Jesus said, "Let your light so shine before men, that they may see your good works and give glory to your Father who is in heaven" (Matt. 5:16). Jesus meant that the only way we can bring glory to God and God's cause is by showing how God has changed our lives and made us able to do lovely things. Jesus' demand was, "What more are you doing than others?" (Matt. 5:47). He strongly condemned the foolishness of the man who heard his words and who did nothing about it (Matt. 7:24-27). He said, "Unless your righteousness exceeds the righteousness of the scribes and Pharisees, you will never enter the Kingdom of heaven" (Matt. 5:20). From all this there can remain no doubt in our minds that the Christian, the citizen of the Kingdom, must be different from other people. We would have known that anyway because the great distinguishing characteristic of the citizen of the Kingdom is that his one aim and desire is to do God's will, whereas the aim of other people is to do their own will.

The Meaning of Faith

This makes us glance briefly at the meaning of two great New Testament words. The first of them is the word faith. We are told often that all that is necessary is that we should have faith. When Paul was miraculously delivered from prison in Philippi, the terrified gaoler asked him, "What must I do to be saved?" And Paul answered, "Believe in the Lord Jesus and you will be saved, you and your household" (Acts 16:31). There are some people who think that that means that all that is necessary is to believe that there are certain things which are true. But there are two kinds of belief. There is what we might call *intellectual belief*; there is a belief which is a belief of the mind and of the mind only. There is what we might call *moral belief*; there is a belief which is a belief not only of the mind but of the whole man. Let us take a simple illustration. I believe that the square of the hypotenuse of a right-angled triangle equals the sum of the squares on the other two sides; but it makes no difference to me; it does not affect my action in the least; true, I believe it with my head, but I stop there. But, I believe that six and six make twelve, therefore I will not pay a shilling and sixpence for two sixpenny bars of chocolate. That belief affects my whole actions in life. Christian faith and belief are far more than things of the head; they do not mean intellectual acceptance of some fact or facts; they mean something which affects a man's whole life. That is what James was getting at when he said, "Faith, if it has no works, is dead." You cannot shew me your faith, he said, apart from your works. Faith without works is dead. And then he went on to use a vivid illustration. He said, the devils are intellectually convinced that there is a God—but for all that they are still devils; it has made no moral difference to them (James 2:17-20). So then we must first be quite sure that a faith which is only a thing of the intellect and the head is not faith in the Christian sense. It must issue in deeds or it is not faith.

Repentance

The second of the great New Testament words is *repentance*. What do we mean when we talk about *repenting*? Most people would answer that when we say, "I repent", we mean, "I am sorry for what I have done." But there is more to it than that, although that answer is half right. In repentance there are four elements. (a) We must realise that what we were doing is wrong. Unless we realise that, we cannot even begin to repent. We can only realise that when we set our lives beside the life of Jesus and see the difference. It is only when we see an expert in action that we know how far we fall short. (b) We must be sorry that we did wrong. That does not always happen. A man may quite well be aware that something he is doing is wrong, but he may be quite defiant about it and not care. (c) We must decide that we will stop the thing. Again that does not always happen. A man may be quite well aware that what he is doing is wrong; he may heartily be sorry for it; and yet he may still go on doing it. Many a man has got a bad habit which he knows is wrong and which he much regrets but which he does not stop. (d) We must actually prove by deeds that our repentance is real and genuine. There is only one way of proving that we are sorry for anything and that is by doing better. It is true that we need Jesus for every step of this. Without him we cannot realise that we ever were wrong; we cannot have in our hearts the true and godly sorrow; we cannot make the decision to change; and least of all can we live the good life. But the one thing that we must see and remember is that repentance does not mean simply being sorry for what we have done; it means proving that sorrow by doing better in the days to come.

Self-respect

We must now ask, Wherein lies the difference between the citizen of the Kingdom and the citizen of the world? What are the qualities which mark out the citizen of the Kingdom? We have already seen how the childlike spirit, the forgiving spirit and the serving spirit are essential passports to the Kingdom, and we need not discuss them again. But in life we have three relationships and the citizen of the Kingdom has something special and extra in regard to all three. First of all, we have a *relationship to ourselves*; and in regard to himself the character-istic of the citizen of the Kingdom is a new self-respect. He gets that self-respect from two things. He gets it from the fact that Jesus believed in him, because Jesus gave him commandments and orders which only a real man can carry out. If Jesus be-lieved that we really could rise to his challenge then there must be something fine in us. And he gets it from the fact that Jesus died for him. If a man's life was worth the sacrifice that God made in Jesus, then it is the most precious thing in the world. These two facts give a man a new self-respect. It means, first, that there are certain things to which a man will no longer stoop. If he is as big a man as Jesus believed him to be and if he is worth that greatest of all sacrifices there are things with which he cannot soil his hands. Once after a terrific battle in the war in which the Brigade of Guards had been involved and out of which they had come terribly battered, an R.A.F. officer met a Guards officer. It was clear to see what an agonis-ing time the Guards officer had been through. The R.A.F. man said, "It must be terrible to belong to the Brigade of Guards because the Guards can never surrender." The traditions, the history, the spirit of the Guards made surrender impossible. Others might surrender and no one would blame them, but not the Guards. They were different. The Christian is different. Others may stoop to certain things; he cannot; his self-respect will not let him. It means, second, that he will never stop on the way on which he has chosen to go. G. K. Chesterton said that the characteristic of a really great man is that he can pass the breaking-point and not break. Others may give up and give in; others may abandon the struggle; the citizen of the Kingdom keeps on when others have stopped. His self-respect will not let him stop.

The new Kindness

Secondly, we have a *relationship to other people*; and in regard to other people the great characteristic of the citizen of the Kingdom is kindness. That kindness obtains in two directions. First, it is kindness of action. In two of his most famous parables Jesus showed this kindness in action. In the parable of the good Samaritan (Luke 10:30-37) the man who is praised is the man who was kind. In the parable of the Sheep and the Goats (Matt. 25:31-46) the whole standard of judgment is how a man acted and behaved towards his fellow men when they were in need. The citizen of the Kingdom must be kinder than anyone else. He will not be able to see anyone in trouble or distress without his heart compelling him to do something about it. Second, it is kindness of judgment. The world is usually very critical and very often tends to think the worst of other people. The strange thing about Jesus was that though he was God's own Son and the best person who ever lived he was not censorious or critical. He was very gentle to the woman taken in adultery when everyone else savagely condemned her (John 8:1-11). No one else would ever have spoken to Peter again after the way in which Peter denied him and let him down; but when Jesus had risen from the dead he sent a very special message to Peter, a message all for himself (Mark 16:7). No true Christian is ever critical and fault-finding, censorious and intolerant. The Salvation Army people tell how once General Booth was marching in a midnight procession through one of the worst and the lowest parts of Glasgow. A girl of the streets, bold and shameless, smiled impudently in his face. The General stepped out of the march and went up to her and put his hand on her shoulder. "My poor child!" he said with infinite compassion in his voice. "My poor child!" Most people would have condemned her out of hand as a loose woman and an evil person, as indeed she was, but all that the General felt was pity; and he was right because the girl was so surprised and so moved that later that evening she came sobbing to the penitent form and found Christ. We live in a hard and a critical world. The citizen of the Kingdom is kind in action and in judgment.

The supreme Loyalty

Thirdly, we have *a relationship to God*. And in regard to God the great characteristic of the citizen of the Kingdom is *loyalty*. Other people may settle what they are going to do from motives of financial gain or personal prestige or their own individual desires and wishes. The question of the Christian is always, What does God want me to do? We must remember that this applies to every moment of life. Going to Church does not make a Christian; Bible reading and prayer do not make a Christian. It is when a man in his home, at work, in his pleasure, in company, alone, everywhere and at all times asks first and foremost, What is God's will for me? and then obeys that will no matter what it costs. Then he is really a citizen of the Kingdom. The Christian must have one loyalty and one only in his life.

Showing Men Jesus

To have this self-respect, this kindness, this loyalty is not going to be easy; but it has got to be done. We must always remember that the great duty of the citizen of the Kingdom is not to talk about Jesus, but actually to show men Jesus in his own life. Someone once said, "A saint is someone in whom Christ lives again." A private soldier said of General Gordon, "I saw God through him." A great bishop made a resolution: "I am anxious to prove, if it please God, in my own life, that the gospels are true." The moral demand of the Kingdom is, in the last analysis, that others should see the reflection of Jesus in us.

The Moral Demand of the Kingdom

The New Testament makes it quite clear that the citizen of the Kingdom must be different. Faith is not faith unless it issues in works. Repentance is not repentance unless it proves its sorrow by its deeds. Towards himself the citizen of the Kingdom must have a self-respect that will neither let him stoop nor stop; towards others he must have kindness of action and kindness of judgment; and towards God he must have a loyalty that nothing can shake; and all through life he must so have Jesus in his heart that men shall see Jesus in his life.

QUESTIONS FOR DISCUSSION

1. What is faith without works?

2. How can we teach ourselves to judge others kindly and not to be critical?

3. If our duty is to show Jesus to others, what kind of life must we live?

12. HINDRANCES TO THE KINGDOM

Hindrances to the Kingdom

Just as there are certain things which are essential passports to entry into the Kingdom of God, so there are certain things which are hindrances and barriers which stop a man from entering into it. Certain of these barriers we must already know for they are the opposites of the things which are the passports to and the necessities of the Kingdom. Just as the childlike, the forgiving and the serving spirit are all necessary passports to the Kingdom, so the proud, the bitter and the selfish spirit are hindrances and barriers to the Kingdom. Just as decision is necessary to entrance to the Kingdom so indecision, the inability to make the decision, is a hindrance and a barrier to it.

The Barrier of Riches

But there is one barrier to the Kingdom about which Jesus was very definite—the barrier of riches. After the rich young ruler had gone sorrowfully away, Jesus turned to his disciples and said, "How hard it will be for those who have riches to enter the Kingdom of God!" The disciples were astonished at this and Jesus went on to say, "It is easier for a camel to go through the eye of a needle than for a rich man to enter the Kingdom of God" (Mark 10:17-27). In the interpretation of the parable of the Sower, the thorns which choked the good seed of the word are equated with the cares of the world and the deceitfulness of riches (Matt. 13:22). Paul insists that we must not trust in what he calls uncertain riches (1 Tim. 6:17). Mammon is a Hebrew word which stands for all wealth, all riches and all material things; and Jesus said, "You cannot serve God and mammon" (Matt. 6:24). It is not so much the possession of riches that the New Testament so consistently condemns. A man may do an immense amount of good with his wealth and may confer the greatest benefits on his fellow-men by the wise and generous use of it. What is condemned is the spirit with which people become immersed in the things of this world, whose one thought, aim, desire and ambition lies in material things.

The true Value of Riches

It is easy to see that riches are not the most important things in the world. There are things that riches cannot buy. They cannot, for instance, buy health; and many a man would trade all his wealth for the good digestion of a penniless boy. Alfred the Great said, "A good name is better than wealth; no sword can slay it; and no rope can bind it." There is an old fable by Æsop like this:

There was a droll of a cobbler who led a life as merry as the day was long, and singing and joking was his delight. But it was not altogether so well with a neighbour of his, though he was a great officer in the Treasury, for there was no singing and hardly any sleeping under his roof; or if he happened to doze a little now and then in a morning it was forty to one the jolly cobbler waked him. How often he wished to himself that sleep could be bought in the market as well as meat and drink. While his head was working on this thought the idea came into his head to send for the cobbler. "Come, neighbour," he said, "you live like a prince here. How much a year do you earn by your trade?" "Faith, sir," said the cobbler, "I keep no account books; but if I can get bread from hand to mouth and finish up even at the year's end, I never trouble myself about to-morrow." "But," said the officer, "if you know what you earn by the day you can easily reckon what it comes to in a year." "Yes," said the cobbler, "that may be so, but we have such a dreadful lot of holidays and festivals and saints' days that it is a mighty hindrance to a poor man who lives by his labour." The dry, blunt way of the cobbler attracted the officer, so he went on, "Come, my friend, you came into my house as a cobbler, what will you say if I send you out of it an emperor?" And he put a purse of a hundred crowns into his hand. "Go your way," he said, "there's an estate for you, and be a good husbander of it." Away went the cobbler with his gold, and in conceit, as rich as if the mines of Peru had been emptied into his lap. Immediately he locked up his gold, and all the comforts of life were locked into the chest with it at the same time. From the time that he was master of this treasure there was no more singing or sleeping in his house; not a cat stirred in the garret, but he cried out that thieves were breaking in. His cottage was so haunted with fears and jealousies and wild alarms that his very life became a burden to him. So after a short time he went back to the officer. "Ah, sir," he said, "if you have any pity for a wretched creature give me back my songs and my sleep and take back your hundred crowns, and a hundred thousand thanks into the bargain."

And Æsop added the moral:

The poor man passes his time merrily, without fear or danger of thieves; but the house that has money in it is as good as haunted.

So the poor man in the fable found that money and riches only brought worry and fear that he would lose them and that he had been far happier without them.

The false Independence

Let us ask now, Why was it that Jesus regarded riches as so dangerous? What was it about riches that made them a danger to the man who would become a citizen of the Kingdom of heaven? For one thing, *riches encourage a false independence.* When a man has plenty of this world's goods he is very apt to come to think that he can deal with life by himself, that he is quite independent, that he needs help from neither man nor God because his money will buy or get him anything that he wishes. Jesus once told a parable about a man like that. He was rich, his fields were so fertile that he had to build bigger barns to hold his grain. He was well satisfied. He did not see that he needed anything. He said to himself, "You have got ample provision made for many days, there is nothing left to worry about. Take your ease, eat, drink and be merry." Because he was prosperous he thought the future was secure and that there was nothing to worry about. And then God said to him, "Fool! This night your soul is required of you." "So," said Jesus, "the value of a man's life has nothing to do with the amount of things which he possesses" (Luke 12:13-21). His riches had made him feel quite independent—and he was quite wrong. The Jews had a saying: "There are three keys which belong only to God—the key of rain, the key of life and the key of death." It is a good thing to earn one's own living and to be able to stand independently on one's own two feet; but it is a foolish thing to think that all the possessions in this world can ever enable us to do without God.

Shackled to this Earth

For another thing, the danger of possessions is that *they shackle a man's thoughts to this earth.* Where our main interest is there our thoughts must mainly be. If all our interests are confined within this earth then we will be interested only in this world and we will forget that there is another world. If we are concerned only with this world we will become so attached to it that we will never want to leave it, that in fact we will consider the coming of death as an unrelieved tragedy. Once Dr. Johnson was shown round one of the greatest and wealthiest estates in England. At the end of it he turned to his companion and said, "These are the things which make it difficult to die." It is true that it is our duty to make the best we can of this life and out of this world, but it is equally true that we must never forget that this world is a stage to another world, that we are not permanent residents here, but only pilgrims and sojourners. There is a danger of getting so involved with this world that we forget that there is another world, and of getting so attached to this world that we never want to leave it.

> "The world is too much with us; late and soon,
>   Getting and spending, we lay waste our powers."

We must never become like that.

The Selfishness of Riches

And lastly, *riches are very apt to beget a selfish view of life*. The odd thing is that the more a man has the more he wants. The Romans used to say, "Riches are like sea-water. The more you drink, the more your thirst is increased." It has been said that enough is always a little more than a man has. One might think that if a man had far more than enough to supply his own needs he would be generous and would be likely to give much away. That does happen when a man is a true Christian and when he loves his fellow-men as God loves them; but far more often the more he has the more he wants, and riches, instead of making him generous, make him more selfish than ever. We must always remember that all that we have is a gift from God. We hold it in trust for him; and therefore we must use it as he would use it. And we know that God so loved that he gave; and we too must so love that we also give.

The Dangers of Riches

It is not wrong to want material things. A man is perfectly right to want enough to support himself and his family in independence and in reasonable comfort. But it is wrong to grow so immersed in the things and the activities of this world that they become our main interest in life and that we never see beyond them. The three great dangers of riches are that they encourage a false independence and we can never be independent of God; they fix our thoughts upon this world and make us forget that there is another world; they tend to make us selfish because it is human nature to want more than we have.

QUESTIONS FOR DISCUSSION

1. At what stage would you say that, from the Christian point of view, a man has more money than he has any right to have?

2. If we want to give away money, are we better to do so personally or through charitable institutions?

3. Is there one law for the rich and another law for the poor in our present society?

PART IV

CHRIST THE KING

1. THE BIRTH AND LIFE OF THE KING

The King

Up until now we have been thinking about the Kingdom. We have seen how the ideas of the Kingdom grew and developed and changed. We have seen the qualities of mind and heart which are the necessary passports of entry into the Kingdom. We have seen the things which are hindrances and barriers which make entry into the Kingdom difficult or even impossible. Now every kingdom must have a king, and so we must now turn our eyes to Jesus, the King of the Kingdom. Before we do this we must be careful to remember one thing. Nothing we could ever say of Jesus would tell the whole story of who Jesus was and what Jesus did. When the writer of the Fourth Gospel came to the end of his story he said, "But there are also many other things which Jesus did; were every one of them to be written, I suppose that the world itself could not contain the books that would be written" (John 21:25). Paul, when he was writing to his friends, spoke of the unsearchable riches of Christ (Eph. 3:8). All we can ever hope to do is to understand only a very little of the wonder of Jesus. In the last analysis, his full wonder is not something about which we read, or something about which someone else tells us; it is something which we must experience and discover for ourselves.

The Birth and the Life of the King

We must begin by thinking of the birth and the life of the King. First, let us try to find a key which will give us a clue as to the meaning of Jesus' life. Who was Jesus and why did he come into the world? Let us remember the definition of the Kingdom of God which has been at the back of our minds all the time—the Kingdom of God is a society upon earth where God's will is as perfectly done as it is in heaven. Now let us listen to some of the things that Jesus said. He said, "My food is to do the will of him who sent me" (John 4:34). He said, "I seek not mine own will, but the will of the Father who hath sent me" (John 5:30). He said, "I came down from heaven not to do my own will, but the will of him who sent me" (John 6.38). When he was faced with the terrible decision in the Garden of Gethsemane, when he had to decide whether to seek escape or to go on and face a cross, he ended by saying "My Father, if this cannot pass me, unless I drink it, thy will be done" (Matt. 26:42). Now remember our definition of the Kingdom of God: and remember how again and again Jesus speaks of his own deliberate and complete obedience to the will of God. We will see at once one of the greatest things Jesus came to do—*He came to show us what the Kingdom is.* He came to demonstrate what a citizen of the Kingdom is and must be. He was the first citizen of the Kingdom; he was the founder of the Kingdom; in him the Kingdom was embodied. Look at him and we will see at once what the Kingdom means and how a citizen of the Kingdom lives.

The Kingdom and God

Now this does not only tell us something about Jesus; it also tells us something tremendous about God. In Jesus, God came down into this world and lived this life exactly as we have to live it. That means that God does not ask us to do anything that he was not prepared to do himself. In this life one of the annoying things is that people very often lay down rules and regulations which they themselves are not prepared to keep. We all do that more or less. We often criticise people for doing the very things we do ourselves. We want people to treat us and to behave to us in a way that very often is quite different from the way we treat them or behave towards them. The trouble about so many of us is that we say, "Do as I say", but we are not able to say, "Do as I do." God is not like that. God laid down the laws of the Kingdom. But God did not stay in heaven in all his peace, his power and his glory and merely watch people trying to carry them out and criticise them when they failed to do so. He came to earth and kept his own laws. He did even more than that. When he did come to earth he did not come to a life that had special advantages. He did not come into a palace or into a wealthy home where things were easy. He came into a village home where life was hard and difficult and where the constant problem of making a living was always to the fore. He came as a tradesman in a carpenter's shop where he had to face all the problems which any working man has to face. God did not claim exemption from life. He took life as we must take it, and under the conditions which we must accept. He kept his own laws of the Kingdom. Chaucer wrote of the poor parson:

> "Christ's love and his apostles twelve
> He taught, but first he followed them himself."

What he taught, he did. Prior, the poet, ended a poem by saying:

> "The truth of what you here lay down
> By some example should be shown."

He declared that it was not enough to speak the truth; if a man was really going to be a good man the truth must be shown in deeds. That is precisely what God did. One of the greatest things about God is that he never demanded from any man what he was not prepared to do and give himself.

An old Fable

This is too great a thing to be illustrated fully by any human story, but there is an old fable of Æsop's which shows what men are so apt to do.

There was, as it seems, an exceedingly clever cat in a certain house, and the mice were so plagued with her at every turn that they called a court to advise upon some way to prevent their being surprised. One member of the board said, "If you will take my advice, there is nothing like hanging a bell round the cat's neck to give warning beforehand when she's coming." They all regarded it as quite the best idea to solve their problem. "Well," said another, "now that we are agreed upon the bell, who will put it round the cat's neck?" But there was no one who would agree to do that and so the whole plan came to nothing.

And the moral Æsop gives at the end is:

The boldest talkers are not always the greatest doers.

Over and over again we command and expect others to do what we are not prepared to do ourselves. God was never like that. He was ready and willing to keep the laws of the Kingdom that he himself had laid down.

A Boy and the Kingdom

If, then, we look at Jesus' life we will see what the Kingdom means for us, what it means to be a citizen of the Kingdom. First, we can see in Jesus *what the Kingdom is for a boy*. We have only one incident of Jesus in the Bible when he was a boy—the time when he was in the Temple when he was twelve years of age—but it tells us all we need to know (Luke 2:41-52). It ends by saying this, "And Jesus went down with them and came to Nazareth, and was obedient to them. . . . And Jesus increased in wisdom and in stature, and in favour with God and man" (Luke 2:51, 52). That tells us three things about Jesus when he was a boy. (a) *He was obedient to his parents*. He was subject to them. God gave us our parents to be our guides in life. We have only to think about all that our parents have done for us. There was a time when we were so little and weak that if we had been neglected even for a week we would have died. There have been all the years when everything we have ever had—food, clothes, a home, pleasure, holidays, schooling,— have been supplied by our parents. No boy can do a worse thing than to bring grief and sorrow to his father and mother. A boy who is on the way to being a citizen of the Kingdom will be obedient to his parents. (b) *He learned new things every day*. He increased in wisdom. It was said of Robert Southey, the great poet, that he was never happy except when he was reading or writing a book. We ought to count it a wasted day when we have not learned something new. Everything we learn is going to stand us in good stead some day. Learning is like amassing a capital which one day will be used to good effect in the business of life. Jesus learned. The boy who will be a citizen of the Kingdom will be a learner all the time. (c) *He pleased God better every day*. He increased in favour with God. That just means that Jesus grew up every day showing more of the splendid character he had and what a fine person he was. Every day we must try to get rid of some fault in our lives and to add some new virtue. One of the sad things in life is that we never seem to get any better. If we have a bad temper we never seem to learn to control it any better. If we are untidy we never seem to get any tidier. If we have a habit of putting things off we never seem any nearer to getting them done on time. It is a most useful thing and often a most humiliating thing to sit down at the end of a week and to say, "Am I any better than I was at the end of last week?" The boy who is on the way to being a citizen of the Kingdom will grow finer and purer and better every day.

> "Leaving every day behind,
>   Something which might hinder;
> Running swifter every day,
>   Growing purer, kinder."

The Kingdom and a Workman

Next we can see in Jesus *what the Kingdom means for a workman*. It was not until he was thirty years of age that Jesus left Nazareth to go out to preach and teach in the towns and villages, by the lakeside, in the hills and on the roads of Palestine (Luke 3:23). From the years of boyhood to early manhood he was the carpenter in Nazareth. That is the way in which people thought of him. When he preached in Nazareth they said, "Is not this the carpenter?" (Mark 6:3). The New Testament tells us nothing about these years, but this we do know—that not a job left that carpenter's shop which was not absolutely perfectly done. One of the most famous things that Jesus ever said was, "My yoke is easy" (Matt. 11:30). The word *easy* can mean in the Greek *well-fitting*. Some people think that that was the sign which was above the door of the carpenter's shop in Nazareth. Shops had signs then just as they have to-day and very likely the sign above Jesus' workroom was "My yokes are made to fit." There is a legend which tells that Jesus of Nazareth made the best ox-yokes in all Galilee and that from all over the country there came people to buy these perfectly made yokes which never galled or irked the necks of the patient oxen. Someone wrote a poem like this:

"If Jesus built a ship, she would travel trim:
  If Jesus roofed a barn, no leaks would be left by him:
  If Jesus planted a garden, he would make it like Paradise:
  If Jesus did my day's work it would delight his Father's eyes."

One of the best ways that we can show that we are citizens of the Kingdom is by doing an honest day's work. There is a tendency nowadays for people to do as little as possible, for them to begin late and stop early, for them to want as much pay as possible for doing as little work as possible, for them to turn out any kind of job so long—as we say—as they can get away with it. Once a man paid a great tribute to a builder. He said, "I bought a house from him and I have discovered that he builds his Christianity into his houses." We must always remember that the citizen of the Kingdom does every job, from the least to the greatest, in such a way that he could take it and offer it to God. He is not thinking of what men would think of it; he is thinking of what God would think of it.

The Kingdom and a Man

Lastly, we can see in Jesus *what the Kingdom means for a man.* In Jesus we see a man living as the only perfect citizen of the Kingdom who ever lived. When we look at him we can see that for a man the Kingdom means two things. (a) *It means service of men.* Jesus said, "The Son of Man came not to be served but to serve" (Mark 10:45). The most amazing thing about Jesus was that he never did anything for his own benefit. Suppose we possessed the powers that Jesus possessed; suppose we had the power to work miracles, how do you think we would use it? There is hardly a person in the world who would not use it to make life easy and comfortable and advantageous for himself. But never at any time did Jesus use any of his powers to get or to gain a single thing for himself. All his life he lived for others. His one question was not, "What can I get? but what can I give?" So, then, the citizen of the Kingdom must all his life think only of what he can do for others. (b) *It means obedience to God.* To be a citizen of the Kingdom means that God's will is our will, for that is the way it was for Jesus all his days. Often Jesus used to go away to be alone with God; before every great act and decision and crisis in his life he prayed. Always he was asking God what God wanted him to do. When we, by his help, forget ourselves and think only of God we, too, will be citizens of the Kingdom.

The Life of the King

In Jesus the Kingdom was fully realised because of all people, he alone perfectly carried out the will of God. In Jesus God came and lived this life and himself fulfilled his own commandments and laws. In Jesus we see that for a boy the Kingdom means obedience, constant growth in knowledge and in goodness, so that we please God better every day. In Jesus we see that for a workman the Kingdom means putting our honest best into every task. In Jesus we see that for a man the Kingdom means serving men and obeying God all the days of his life.

QUESTIONS FOR DISCUSSION

1. Is it possible in modern industrial conditions to work as a Christian ought to work?

2. What does it mean to serve men. How can we in our lives render this Christian service?

3. What can we do to enable us to grow in knowledge and in character all through life?

2. THE DEATH AND SACRIFICE OF THE KING

The inevitable Cross

When the Roman gladiators entered the arena to fight with the wild beasts, before their struggle, they turned to the assembled crowd in the amphitheatre and said, *Te morituri salutamus*—We who are about to die salute you. In one sense it is true to say that Jesus came into the world to die. Holman Hunt painted a famous picture. It shows the young Jesus standing at the door of the carpenter's shop in Nazareth. He has been working at some job and he is tired. It is late afternoon and the westering sun is slanting low through the door. And as Jesus stands at the door he stretches wide his arms, as a man will to ease his tired muscles after cramped work. As he does so the sun casts his shadow on the wall behind and it is the shadow of the cross. In the corner of the picture you can see Mary catch a glimpse of that shadow and you can see the pain and sorrow in her eyes. In one sense it is true to say that that picture is symbolically true, because all his life Jesus lived under the shadow of the Cross. But here we must enter one word of warning. Although Jesus' death was so all-important that does not mean that his death is the only thing that matters. His life is of equal importance, for this very simple and yet completely compelling reason—it was the loveliness, the sinlessness, the perfect submission of that life to God that gave his death its value. It was not a man who had lived an ordinary sinful life who died on the Cross; it was not even a man good by the world's standards who died there; it was a man who had lived the very life of God among men who died there. It was precisely his life which gave his death its supreme value. Had he not been who and what he was in life, his death would have lost the value that it had.

A Death expected

As we read the story of Jesus in the gospels, two things become crystal clear. First, *Jesus expected to die*. The fact that he had to die came as no surprise to him; he was well aware of it from the beginning to end. When Jesus was baptised by John the Baptist God's voice came to him and he heard God saying, "Thou art my beloved Son; with thee I am well pleased" (Mark 1:11). That saying is composed of two texts from the Old Testament. "Thou art my beloved Son"—that is Ps. 2:7; and that was a text which every Jew took as referring to the Messiah, the conquering King who was to come. "With thee I am well pleased"—that is from Is. 42:1; it is a description of the Servant of the Lord whose portrait culminates in Is. 53 which tells of one who was wounded for our transgressions and bruised for our iniquities. Therefore right from the beginning Jesus foresaw that he would conquer, that he was King of the Kingdom; but he also foresaw—God told him—that he must suffer and die. Immediately after Peter had made his great discovery that Jesus was the Son of God, Jesus said to him and to the other disciples that he must go to Jerusalem and suffer many things and be killed and rise again (Matt. 16:13-21). Soon after the glory of the mountain of transfiguration Jesus again told his disciples that he would be betrayed into the hands of men, that they would kill him and that he would rise again (Matt. 17:22, 23). When James and John had shown their worldly ambitions in their request for the chief places in the coming Kingdom, Jesus tried to show them that his way was the way of service and not of power; and he finished by saying, "The Son of Man came . . . to give his life as a ransom for many" (Mark 10:35-45). It is abundantly clear that Jesus' death came to him as no shock. He never expected anything else. Therein lies his matchless courage. At any moment he might have turned aside and taken an easier way, but he went fearlessly and unflinchingly on knowing what the end would be. Many a man in a sudden moment of heroism when a crisis of danger came unexpectedly on him has behaved like a hero; but it is a far harder thing to see some terrible thing coming for years and to nerve oneself to go on and meet it. A certain novelist tells of two children talking. The one says to the other, when they are talking about the games they play, "Do you ever pretend when you are going along the road that there is something terrible waiting for you round the corner and that you have got to go and face it? It makes it so exciting." Jesus did not pretend; he knew what was waiting for him.

A voluntary Death

The second thing that the New Testament makes crystal clear about the death of Jesus is that *Jesus chose to die*. By the side of the road between Burntisland and Kinghorn there is a monument to Alexander III of Scotland with this inscription: "To the Illustrious Alexander III, the last of Scotland's Celtic Kings, who was accidentally killed near this spot, March XIX MCCLXXXVI; erected on the six-centenary of his death." Here was a king who was *accidentally* killed. Jesus did not die either by accident or by compulsion. His death was entirely voluntary and of his own free will. Jesus said, "I lay down my life . . . No one takes it from me, but I lay it down of my own accord" (John 10:17, 18). When Peter sought to intervene in the Garden of Gethsemane and to contest the arrest of Jesus, Jesus told him to put up his sword. He said, "Do you think that I cannot appeal to my Father, and he will at once send me more than twelve legions of angels?" (Matt. 26:51-53; cp. John 18:6-11). There is a story of a young French soldier who was badly wounded in the arm. He was a splendid specimen of humanity physically, and the surgeon, much against his will, and after every effort to save it, had to amputate his arm. He came to the bedside of the young soldier to await his return to consciousness so that he could break the news to him as gently and as sympathetically as possible. When the soldier came to himself, the surgeon said, "My boy, I am very sorry to tell you that you have lost your arm." The lad answered, "I did not lose it: I gave it—for France." Jesus did not lose His life. His death happened neither by an accident nor by a compulsion. To the end he could have kept his life had he so chosen. He gave it of his own free will.

The last Loyalty

What, then, does this death of the King show to us? For one thing, *it shows us the length to which loyalty must go*. Remember that citizenship of the Kingdom demands perfect obedience to the will of God. Remember that Jesus was the first and the perfect citizen of the Kingdom. Jesus' loyalty to the will of God went the length of the Cross. He was faithful —*unto death*. The great question in life is—Unto what are we faithful and loyal to God? Up to what point does our loyalty extend? People may be loyal to God so long as that loyalty does not impinge on their comfort or their popularity or their ease or their pleasure. They may be faithful to God within the Church building or when they are with other Christian people; and they may forget their loyalty outside the Church or when they are in company which makes that loyalty difficult. There is a famous picture of an incident which happened when the volcano erupted and buried the Roman city of Pompeii under the molten lava. It shows everyone fleeing in disordered terror for their lives; but it shows a Roman soldier standing at his post. There is horror in his eyes as he sees the advancing tide of death; but he will not leave his post. He has been told to stand there and he will obey his orders even if these orders mean death; and the title of the picture is *Faithful unto Death*. Jesus obeyed God even when that obedience meant death. The citizens of the Kingdom will be loyal to God no matter what that loyalty costs. No kingdom can be built on citizens who are loyal when things go well and who abandon their loyalty when things grow difficult. In every kingdom and above all in the Kingdom of heaven it is the loyalty which is true through thick and thin which matters.

"I vow to thee my country—all earthly things above—
Entire and whole and perfect, the service of my love—
The love that asks no questions, the love that stands the test,
That lays upon the altar the dearest and the best;
The love that never falters, the love that pays the price,
The love that makes undaunted the final sacrifice."

If that is the love that a man bears to his country, how much more must he bear it to the Kingdom of God?

The utter Love

But further, *the death of Jesus shows us the length to which God's love will go*. Remember, God was in Jesus. It would have been a great thing if God had come down to live our life in this world in an ordinary way. It would have been a still greater thing if God had shown that all his power was used to help sick and sad, suffering and hungry men and women. But the greatest thing of all is that God not only came to earth, not only used his power for the sake of men, but in the end gave his life for men. This proves that quite literally there is no limit to the love of God. If Jesus had stopped before the Cross it would have proved that God was willing to do a great deal for men, but that there was a limit beyond which God would not go. But when Jesus went right on to the Cross it shows us that there is literally nothing which God will not do and bear for men. When we look at the Cross it says to us, "God loved you enough to bear and to suffer that for you." There is a love which is known as *cupboard love*; that is, the kind of love whose aim and object is to get something out of the person it declares it loves. There is a love which is true enough so long as no great demands are made upon it; but which flickers and dies if there is any need for sacrifice to be made. It is when we are in trouble and when we have to call upon our friends for help that we know who our real friends are. It is then that the false love and the false friends slip away and leave us. But the death of Jesus proves that there are no lengths and no depths to which the love of God for man will not go. And a love like that demands that we love him as he first loved us.

A Death for us

And lastly, *the death of Jesus was for us*. Of the suffering servant Isaiah said, "The Lord has laid on him the iniquity of us all" (Is. 53:6). It is told that once a missionary was giving a show of lantern slides of the life of Christ in an Indian village. He was showing them in the open air on a warm dark night with the whitewashed wall of a house as his screen. One by one the scenes in Jesus' life were depicted. At last there came the slide which showed the Cross; and as the picture shone upon the screen, an Indian, as if by a compulsion he could not help, rose from his place and came forward with hands outstretched. "Come down from that Cross," he said, "that is my place, not yours." It must always remain true that if God dealt with us as we deserve there could be nothing but punishment. If we were treated according to our deserts we could never become citizens of the Kingdom of God because none of us has ever fully obeyed the will of God; we would be forever shut out. But Jesus on the Cross bore the punishment that should have fallen on us. Dr. James Stewart tells that when the emissaries of the African chief came upon Bishop Hannington of Uganda to murder him, Hannington said, "Tell the king that I open up the road to Uganda with my life." It was because he had pioneers like him ready to die that the road was opened up. And Jesus could say, "Tell all men that I open up the road to God and into the Kingdom with My life."

> "There was no other good enough
>   To pay the price of sin;
> He only could unlock the gate
>   Of heaven, and let us in."

The Death and Sacrifice of the King

Jesus knew he had to die and yet he never turned back. Jesus was not compelled to die; he chose to die. By his death he shows the lengths to which loyalty to God's will must go. By his death he shows the length that God's love will go and that there is no limit to what God's love will do for man. By his death he bore the punishment that men should have borne and so opened up the door to God and to the Kingdom that all may go in.

QUESTIONS FOR DISCUSSION

1. What do you think that men would do to Jesus if he came to earth as a man today?

2. It has been said that the Cross shows the length to which man's sin will go, and the length to which God's love will go. Discuss this.

3. What could we have known, and what could we never have known, about God, if Jesus had not come into this world and lived and died?

3. THE RESURRECTION AND THE VICTORY OF THE KING

General Introduction

This is of necessity a long chapter. In a general handbook it is sufficient to deal with the Resurrection under one of its many aspects. But in a book the specific purpose of which it is to discuss the King and the Kingdom and especially in a section wherein we study the King himself, we must take as complete a view as the limits of such a work as this will allow. For that reason we will look at the Resurrection and the victory of the King under four great heads. First, we will look at it *as a historical fact*, for there will always be many who require their faith in the fact of the Resurrection buttressed and strengthened. Second, we will look at it *as it affects God* and God's governance of this world. Third, we will look at it *as it affects Jesus himself*. And fourth, we will look at it *as it affects ourselves*.

The historical Fact of the Resurrection

The Resurrection is the most important single fact in the whole Christian religion. It is so for this simple yet all-important reason. Had there been no Resurrection we would never have heard of the Cross. Had there been no Easter Day we would never have heard of Good Friday. The attitude of the disciples after the crucifixion is clear. They were broken men. Their dream was gone. Their hopes had crashed. There was nothing left to do but to go back to the old life and to try to forget. When Jesus met the two men on the Emmaus road they said something that summed the whole thing up. They told him how they had loved Jesus, how they had built their hopes on him and then there comes the wistful, poignant, tragic, hopeless, pessimistic saying, "But we had hoped that he was the one to redeem Israel" (Luke 24:21). In that saying there is all the pathos of shattered hopes. There was nothing left to do but to try to forget this interlude with Jesus and to go back to the old life and the old ways with the admission that all their expectations had come to nothing. It was the Resurrection which changed all that. It was the discovery that Jesus was not dead, but most gloriously alive that convinced the disciples that so far from having come to the end of the road they were standing on the threshold of a new life of the like of which they had never dreamed. Clearly the Resurrection is the most important of all historical events because without it there would never have been any such thing as a Christian faith. We must, therefore, begin by convincing ourselves that the Resurrection did actually happen, and by equipping ourselves to give a reason to those who seek to say that it did not.

The empty Tomb

We may start with one fact which is as well authenticated and as certain as any fact in history can ever be—the fact that on the first Easter morning *the tomb where Jesus had been laid was empty*. The evidence for the fact of the empty tomb is overwhelming. The sceptics have tried to explain away the empty tomb in different ways. (a) They have suggested that Jesus never really died, that he fainted on the Cross, that he came to himself and revived in the cool of the tomb, that he succeeded in escaping from the tomb, and came to his own people again and claimed to have risen from the dead. Consider what that involves. Jesus had been scourged (John 19:1). When a man was scourged under Roman law he was bound in a kneeling position so that his naked back was exposed. The lash was a long leather thong studded at intervals with pieces of sharp bone and lead which literally tore a man's back into strips. Many a man had died under the lash; still more had lost their reason and emerged raving mad; few retained consciousness to the end of that bitter ordeal; and all who survived were broken men. Jesus staggered under the weight of his cross so that they impressed Simon of Cyrene to carry it for him (Mark 15:21). They nailed him to the Cross and in the end one of the soldiers thrust his spear into Jesus' side and there came out water and blood which was the sign quite literally of a broken heart (John 19:34). They prepared his body for the tomb. That meant that they anointed it with spices and wrapped it in yards of linen strips. They laid it in the rock tomb. Across the opening of such tombs there ran in a groove a great circular stone like a cartwheel. When the women were coming to visit the tomb one of the things that puzzled them was how they were going to move the stone at all (Mark 16:3). Put all these things together. Suppose Jesus had survived the Cross, suppose he had survived the spear thrust, how could he possibly have freed himself from the linen wrappings? How could he possibly have moved the stone, and that from inside the tomb? If he had emerged, would he not have emerged a figure so battered and broken as to be almost helpless, instead of a figure of glory as he was? Simply on the facts of the case it is easier to believe that Jesus rose from the dead than that afterwards he escaped from the tomb without having died at all.

(b) They have suggested that the Jews stole Jesus' body away lest his grave become the shrine of a martyr and lest his influence should continue even after he was dead. If the Jews had done that surely they would have been the first to say so. Early preaching was essentially the preaching of the Resurrection. No Christian sermon was ever preached which did not stress the fact of the Resurrection (cp. Acts 2:24, 32; 3:15, 26; 4:10, 33; 5:30; 10:40; 13:30, 33, 34; 17:31). Nothing would have been easier for the Jews than to disprove the Resurrection if they themselves had removed the body. Had they done so they would most certainly have said so because by saying so they could have discredited the Christian preachers once, finally and for all.

(c) They have suggested that the disciples removed the body and then falsely claimed that Jesus rose from the dead. By A.D. 70 all the disciples were dead except John; and, as far as we know, all died martyrs' deaths. It seems completely incredible that men should die for what they *knew* to be a lie. It seems beyond all belief that if they themselves had fabricated the Resurrection they would be prepared to die for the truth of the Resurrection. No doubt a man might die for a dream and delusion, but not for a lie which he himself had taken part in concocting.

(d) They have suggested that the whole thing was an illusion and a hallucination, that the disciples did genuinely believe that Jesus had risen from the dead, but that they believed this in consequence of some imaginary vision which had come to their half-crazed minds. Two plain facts explode that theory beyond repair. (1) Hallucinations come to a person who is conditioned to expect them; and the last thing the disciples ever expected was the Resurrection. In fact, they were quite certain that Jesus was finally dead. No body of men were ever less likely to have such a hallucination. (2) That first ten men (John 20: 19-21), then eleven men (John 20:26-29) and then about five hundred men (1 Cor. 15:6) should all have the same hallucination at one and the same time is so improbable that it can justly be said to be impossible. Had the fact of the Resurrection depended on the evidence of one or two people to whom Jesus had appeared separately the theory of hallucination might have to be considered; but in light of the fact that he appeared to whole groups and even crowds of men the theory of hallucination becomes untenable.

The divergent Accounts

It is further argued that the fact that the gospels give divergent accounts of the Resurrection is proof that it did not happen. The Resurrection appearances are as follows:—

1. To Mary Magdalene (Mark 16:9, 10; John 20:14).
2. To the women returning home (Matt. 28:9).
3. To two disciples on the way to Emmaus (Mark 16:12; Luke 24:13-31).
4. To Peter (Luke 24:34).
5. To ten apostles in the upper room (Luke 24:36; John 20:19).
6. To eleven apostles in the upper room (John 20:26).
7. To the disciples by the lakeside (John 21:1-24).
8. To five hundred brethren at once (1 Cor. 15:6).
9. To James (1 Cor. 15:7).
10. The Ascension (Luke 24:50, 51).

If we study these passages we see that the differences are negligible. To take but one—the messenger at the tomb changes from gospel to gospel. In Mark 16:5 the messenger is a young man. In Luke 24:4 it is two men in shining garments.

In Matt. 28:2 it is the angel of the Lord. In John 20:12 it is two angels. Now nothing can be made of differences like that. The one fact that does not vary is the fact of the Resurrection itself. And surely this must remain true—the very fact that there are divergences in the accounts of the Resurrection is the best guarantee of their sincerity and their truth. Had the accounts of all the four gospels dovetailed with complete accuracy and without divergence in the smallest detail we might well have assumed that there had been some manipulating of the records. It is an insurmountable fact that no two eye-witnesses of any event will give precisely the same account of it. And therefore no one need be in the least troubled by the little differences in the four accounts, because through them all the one great fact of the empty tomb and the Risen Lord stands fast.

The Existence of the Church

But the greatest proof of the Resurrection is simply the existence of the Church. In the hours when Jesus was on trial we see Peter abjectly denying his Lord (Luke 22:54-62). Mark, with bleak brevity, writes, after the arrest in the garden, "They all forsook Him, and fled" (Mark 14:50). John draws us a vivid picture of the disciples meeting behind locked doors in terror lest their turn should be next (John 20:19). The whole picture is one of men in terror and in despair. And just seven weeks later we find these very same disciples proclaiming the name of Jesus in Jerusalem without fear and defying the Sanhedrin to do its worst (Acts 4:19, 20). Every effect must have an adequate cause and the cause which turned cowards into heroes, and men who met behind locked doors into men who blazoned forth Jesus' name in the market place was the Resurrection. On the Resurrection the Church was founded; without it the Church would never have existed. The very fact of the Church is the proof of the Resurrection.

The Resurrection as a Fact

We may without hesitation accept the Resurrection as a historical fact. The attempts to explain it away produce far more difficulties than they solve. The divergences in the accounts of it are but a guarantee of good faith. The existence of the Church cannot be explained in any other way than by the fact of the Resurrection.

The Resurrection and God

The Resurrection tells us something about God and about God's governance of this world. It tells us something about the very constitution of this world and about the very principles on which this world is founded. Paul declared roundly that if there is no Resurrection then our faith is vain (1 Cor. 15:14). Why should that be? Why is the Resurrection so essential to our faith in God?

The Triumph of Goodness

For one thing, the Resurrection is the proof that in the end *goodness is stronger than evil.* The sin of man took Jesus and crucified him. That is to say sin took the loveliest and the best person who ever lived in this world and nailed him to a cross. If that had been the end it would have meant that sin is stronger than goodness and can defeat it; but the Resurrection is the final proof that in the end goodness is stronger than sin. The Romans had a saying, "Great is the truth and in the end it will prevail." All history is in the end the proof of that. We have only to ask ourselves, Whether would you rather be Socrates who was condemned or the judges who condemned him? Whether would you rather be Paul who was executed or Nero who found him guilty? Whether would you rather be one of the Christian martyrs or one of the persecutors who hounded them to the cross, the stake and the wild beasts? Over and over again the cause for which men died has been the cause which did prevail in the long run. As Fosdick had it, Nero condemns Paul to death but the centuries pass on and men call their sons Paul and their dogs Nero. J. R. Lowell, the American poet, has a poem on this apparent defeat but ultimate triumph of what is right:

"Once to every man and nation comes the moment to
    decide,

In the strife of Truth with Falsehood, for the good or
    evil side;
Some great cause, God's new Messiah, offering each the
    bloom or blight
Parts the goats upon the left hand and the sheep upon the
    right,
And the choice goes by forever 'twixt that darkness and
    that light.
Careless seems the great Avenger, history's pages but
    record
One death-grapple in the darkness 'twixt old systems and
    the Word;
Truth forever on the scaffold, Wrong forever on the
    throne,
Yet that scaffold sways the future, and behind the dim
    unknown,
Standeth God within the shadow, keeping watch above
    His own."

There is an eastern faith called Zoroastrianism. It depicts
all this universe as a continual struggle between the god of the
light and the god of the dark; and that which determines a
man's destiny is the side which he takes. Again and again the
low way of the dark seems easy; and the high way of the light
seems hard; but in the end there is only one way to victory.
This is an intensely personal thing. It means that every time
we choose the hard right and reject the easy wrong we are doing
what Jesus did. It may be that at the moment we suffer; but
the Resurrection is the proof that the man who chooses the
right way has put himself on the victor's side because the Resurrection is the proof that goodness is always stronger than evil.

The Triumph of Life

Further, the Resurrection is the proof that *life is stronger than
death*. The Jews crucified Jesus; they knew him to be walled
up in the rock tomb; they stood back and said, "That is the end
of him; he is eliminated now." But life was stronger than death
and Jesus rose again. In the wartime there was a church in
London which was all set out to keep the harvest thanksgiving
service on the Sunday. In the middle of the display there was a

sheaf of corn. But on the Saturday night there came a terrible air-raid and on the Sunday morning that church was a heap of ruins and there was no harvest thanksgiving that Sunday. The months passed on, the winter ended, and the spring came. And on the bomb site where the church had stood there emerged a patch of shoots of green; and all summer they grew until in the autumn there was a flourishing patch of corn growing there. It was the seeds of the sheaf of corn which had sown themselves. Not all the bombs and rubble and ruins could end the life that was in the corn. Life is always stronger than death. We will return to this; but at the moment it is enough to remember that Jesus said, "Because I live, you will live also" (John 14:19). We must always be quite sure that even though death looks like the end life is stronger than death and life can conquer even death.

The Triumph of Love

Still further, the Resurrection is the proof that *love is stronger than hate*. The people who crucified Jesus stood for hate. Jesus was love itself. He was the very love of God come down to men. The hate of men took that love and crucified it and thought that they had killed it forever, but that love rose again and conquered hate. Love is always stronger than hate. It is the only thing that can kill hate. If someone hates us and we hate that person in return, then hate grows stronger and stronger. But if we refuse to hate and if we will not cease loving, then in the end even hate can be conquered by love. There is a very beautiful poem which sums the matter up:

> I heard two soldiers talking as they came down the hill,
> The sombre hill of Calvary, bleak and black and still.
> And one said, "The night is late, these thieves take long
> to die."
> And one said, "I am sore afraid, and yet I know not why."
>
> I heard two women weeping as down the hill they came
> And one was like a broken rose, and one was like a flame.
> One said, "Men shall rue this deed their hands have done."
> And one said only through her tears, "My son, my son,
> my son!"

I heard two angels singing ere yet the dawn was bright;
And they were clad in shining robes, robes and crowns of
light.
And one sang, "Death is vanquished," and one in golden
voice
Sang, "Love hath conquered, conquered all, O heaven
and earth rejoice!"

Ultimately the lesson of the Resurrection is that love has
conquered all.

The Resurrection and God

The Resurrection of Jesus tells us that in God's governance
of this world goodness is always stronger than evil; life is
always stronger than death; and love is always stronger than
hate.

Jesus and the Resurrection

We have looked at the fact of the Resurrection. We have
looked at the Resurrection as it reacts on our belief in God.
Now we come to look at the Resurrection in regard to Jesus.
One thing any careful reading of the gospels makes clear—that
Jesus never foretold his death without foretelling his Resurrection. When Peter had made his great discovery and confession and when Jesus had shocked his disciples by following
up that confession with the immediate foretelling of his Cross
and shame, he ends his prophecy in the words "and be raised
again the third day" (Matt. 16:21). When he set out on his last
journey to Jerusalem once again he warned his disciples of
the terrible things that lay ahead; and then after the dread
warning he added the phrase, "and he will be raised on the
third day" (Matt. 20:18-19). Always Jesus regarded his death
not as the end, but as the prelude to his glory.

The Vindication of Jesus

Because of that repeated statement of Jesus that after his
sufferings he would rise again, first and foremost *the Resurrection was for Jesus a vindication.* It once, finally and for all proved
him right; it proved that he was not deluded, but that all his

beliefs concerning himself were fully justified. Studdert Kennedy has a poem in which he imagines the scene as Jesus died on the Cross while the soldiers beneath the Cross cast lots for his garments:

> And sitting down they watched Him there, the soldiers did.
> There, while they played at dice, He made His sacrifice,
> And died upon His Cross to rid God's world of sin.
> He was a gambler, too, my Christ. He took His life and threw
> It for a world redeemed. And ere the agony was done
> Before the westering sun went down, crowning that day with its crimson crown.
> *He knew that He had won.*

But that sense of victory might well have been a delusion. The proof that it was not a delusion was the Resurrection. First and foremost, the Resurrection was the vindication of Jesus. It justified his every claim. It proved him unanswerably to be not a deluded man but in very truth the Son of God. It is told that it had been arranged that after the Battle of Waterloo, the result of the battle was to be relayed to England by a series of semaphore signals. So the signals were sent and in time came to England. The watchers saw the signal go up. It read: WELLINGTON DEFEATED. And at the sight of that the hearts of the waiting watchers sank within them. And then to these two words another was added: WELLINGTON DEFEATED ENEMY. What looked like defeat was turned into victory and men's hearts rejoiced. That is exactly what the Resurrection did for Jesus. The Cross, the first half of the message, looked like blank defeat. The Resurrection, the second half of the message, turned the defeat into flaming victory.

The Liberation of Jesus

But further, *the Resurrection was uniquely the liberation of Jesus.* Jesus had come with the message that God so loved *the world.* And yet so far as we know he was only once outside the boundaries of Palestine (Matt. 15:21). Palestine at its greatest extent is only about 120 miles from north to south and 40 miles from east to west. So here was Jesus with a message for the world confined to this little strip of territory. His bodily presence could come to so few; his voice could reach so few; and yet he had a message for all mankind. So long as he was in the body that was inevitable for he was subject to all the limitations of the body. But the Resurrection set him free from all bodily limitations and meant that his presence could be with all men and his words could personally reach every heart. In one of his plays John Masefield tells how Pilate's wife was anxious to know what had happened to Jesus for she had been sure that he should never have been condemned (Matt 27:19). Her name was Procula. She sent for Longinus, the centurion who had been in charge of the crucifixion and who had ended on his knees before the Cross (Matt. 27:54), and she asked him what had happened. A dialogue somewhat like this ensued. "He was a fine young fellow," said Longinus, "but when we were finished with him, he was a poor broken thing upon a Cross." "So you think," said Procula, "that he is finished and his work is ended," "No madam," said Longinus, "I do not." "What then?" said Procula. And Longinus answered, "He is set free throughout the world where neither Jew nor Greek can stop his truth." That is precisely what the Resurrection did for Jesus. His death, so far from ending his work, set him free to do his work. When he was in the body he was cribbed and confined to the one place and to the one circle of people. When he was risen he was set free throughout all the world to come to every man and to speak to every man.

The Resurrection of Jesus

For Jesus the Resurrection was a vindication of his every claim and a final proof that he was not a deluded enthusiast but the Son of God. It was his liberation whereby, set free from the limitations of the body, he was enabled to act on all men throughout all the world.

The Resurrection and ourselves

We have looked at the fact of the Resurrection; at the Resurrection as it reflects to us the very nature of God's governance of the world; as it affected Jesus himself. Now there is no single event or incident in Jesus' life which is without its meaning and its significance for us. So, finally, we must ask the question: What is the effect of the Resurrection for us?

The End of Death's Terror

First, the Resurrection means for us that *the fear of death is gone.* Instinctively men have always feared death. When Dr. Johnson was asked if the fear of death was not natural to men, he answered that is was so much so that life was one long effort not to think about it. A famous American journalist set at the very head of his own personal creed the resolution, "Never to allow myself to think of death." Even when men did not fear death they felt that in it there was a terrible finality. It was the closing of a door which was never to open again and a door which led into the dark. Once H. G. Wells made a speech to the P.E.N. club. He was within a few days of his seventieth birthday and he was already the author of some eighty-five books at least. In that speech he said, "I feel as though I were still in the nursery playing with my nicest toys, and nurse opens the door and says, 'Come now, George, it's bedtime; put these toys away.' Well, it will soon be time to put these toys away and there is still so much to be done." He regarded death as an end and a conclusion. R. L. Stevenson wrote a beautiful but grim four lines:

> "I have trod the upward and the downward slope;
> I have endured and done in days before;
> I have hoped for all and bade farewell to hope;
> And I have lived and loved and closed the door."

He regarded death as the closing and the closed door. Walter Savage Landor, thinking of the approach of death, wrote some lines:

> "I strove with none, for none was worth my strife;
> Nature I loved, and after nature, art;
> I warmed both hands before the fire of life;
> It sinks, and I am ready to depart."

He regarded death as the dying of the fire and the going out into the cold. But the Christian has the utter and the absolute certainty that Jesus conquered death; that he rose again; and that he himself will share in that victory. For the Christian the Resurrection is not only the defeat of death for Jesus; it is the defeat of death for him, too. And, therefore, the reaction of the Christian to death is quite different. When F. B. Meyer, that great saint and preacher, received the sentence of death, he wrote a little note to a friend like this:

"I have just heard to my surprise that I have only a few more days to live. It may be that before this reaches you I shall have entered the palace. Don't trouble to write; we shall meet in the morning."

The difference is obvious. For Meyer death was not the dark, but the King's Palace; not the night, but the dawn. A famous author wrote a poem about a young man who had been killed, as it seemed, all too soon.

"I stood beside your new-made grave,
And as I mused my sorrow fled,
Save for these mortal thoughts that crave
For sight of those whom men call dead.
I knew you moved in ampler powers,
A warrior in a purer strife,
Walking that world that shall be ours
When death has called us dead to life.
The rough white cross above your breast,
The earth ungraced by flower or stone
Are bivouac marks of those that rest
One instant ere they hasten on.
More fit such graves, than funeral pile,
Than requiem dirge, than ballad strain;
I'll lay me down and bleed awhile,
And then I'll rise and fight again."

For a man like that death is the gateway to life and a greater life than ever this world had to offer. The consequence of the Resurrection is that we need neither fear death for ourselves nor sorrow for the death of others. As Ruskin said, "I will

not wear black for the guests of God." An American poetess
who had lost someone very dear to her wrote:

> Shall I wear mourning for my soldier dead?
> I—a believer? Give me red,
> Or give me royal purple for the king
> At whose high court my love is visiting.
> Dress me in green for growth, for life made new;
> For skies his dear feet march, dress me in blue;
> In white for his white soul; robe me in gold
> For all the pride that his new rank shall hold.
> In earth's dim gardens blooms no hue too bright
> To dress me for my love who walks in light.

For us, the first meaning of the Resurrection is that death
is swallowed up in victory.

The Risen Presence

Secondly, the great meaning of the Resurrection for the life
of every day, apart altogether from death, is that *Jesus is always
with us*. That is the root difference between Jesus and all other
heroic figures. They lived and died. We read about them; we
study their lives; we hear stories about them. But we actually
meet and experience Jesus and every day in life we live actually
in his presence.

> "Shakespeare is dust, and will not come
> To question from his Avon tomb,
> And Socrates and Shelley keep
> An Attic and Italian sleep.
> They see not. But, O Christians, who
> Throng Holborn and Fifth Avenue,
> May you not meet, in spite of death,
> A traveller from Nazareth?"

Francis Thompson wrote in a famous poem about the
presence of Jesus when things were difficult:

> "But (when so sad thou canst not sadder)
> Cry;— and upon thy so sore loss
> Shall shine the traffic of Jacob's ladder
> Pitched betwixt heaven and Charing Cross.

> Yea, in the night, my Soul, my daughter,
> Cry,—clinging Heaven by the hems;
> And lo, Christ walking on the water
> Not of Gennesareth, but Thames!"

For us the great lesson of the Resurrection is that Jesus is as really present here today just as he was in Palestine long ago.

The Inspiration and the Warning

To us that must mean two things. First, *it must be an inspiration*. It means that we are never left to do anything alone. There is an unwritten saying of Jesus, a saying that is not in any of the gospels, but which was discovered in an old manuscript found in Egypt. Jesus said, "Cleave the wood and you will find me; raise the stone and I am there." The meaning is that as the mason chisels the stone and as the carpenter cuts the wood Jesus is there. The Resurrection means that no matter what task we have to do Jesus is there to do it with us. Second, *it must be a warning*. It means that we are given the task of making all life fit for him to see. If we are playing a game, if we are giving some performance, the more distinguished the audience the more we wish and the more we will strive to do well. The teams at Wembley, the artistes at a command performance will strive doubly hard to put up a good show when the Queen is there. All life is lived in the presence of the King of kings. Surely that must mean that we must never do anything that would grieve him to look upon. Sometimes we say, or at least we think, no one will see me do this, so it does not matter. No human person may see—but Jesus does. Sometimes we say, What would happen if Jesus came to stay in our house? Lady Acland tells how once her little daughter had one of those bursts of temper that we all have. After the storm was over she and the little girl were sitting on the stairs together making things up and the little girl looked up and said, "Mother, I wish Jesus would come and stay in this house and then we wouldn't be cross any more." But Jesus *is* here! everything we do is done in his presence.

The Presence of Jesus

Margaret Avery, the expert on religious education, tells of an incident that happened in a north country school. The teacher had been teaching the incident of Jesus stilling the storm. As the school finished one winter day soon after, there came a blizzard of wind and snow. The teacher was helping the young children home. They were in real peril. She had almost to drag them through the driving snow. As they struggled on she suddenly heard one little boy say, "We could be doing with that chap Jesus now." He was right. There are many times in life when we could be doing with Jesus here; and the meaning of the Resurrection is that he is here, that his promise is true, that he is with us always even unto the end of the world.

The Resurrection and ourselves

For us the Resurrection means that death has no more fears and no more terrors, that it is in fact the gateway to life. It means that Jesus is always with us; and the fact of his presence should be an inspiration to do well and a warning to keep us from doing anything that we would be ashamed that he should see.

QUESTIONS FOR DISCUSSION

1. Why is it so important to be sure of the Resurrection?

2. Can you be a Christian without believing in life after death?

3. What does the Resurrection mean for us?

4. THE FINAL TRIUMPH OF THE KING

The Christian View of History

There have been many different viewpoints from which history has been regarded. It has been said that history is the record of the sins, the follies and the mistakes of men. That view regards history as nothing other than a long account of the blunders and the crimes of men. H. G. Wells said, "Man who

began in a cave behind a wind-break will end in the disease-
soaked ruins of a slum." That view regards history as an inevitable progress to final disaster. The Stoics believed that
history endlessly repeated itself. They believed that history was
circular. Once every three thousand years or so, they held, the
world went up in a great conflagration and then it was reborn
and began all over again and the very same things were said
and done and the very same events repeated themselves. That
view regards history as a kind of treadmill; it regards history
as going round in ever-repeated circles and getting nowhere at
all. The whole essence of the Christian view of history is that
history is quite definitely going somewhere, that it has a goal,
that it will have a consummation, and that that goal and consummation find their realisation in the perfect reign of God
and the return of Jesus Christ in the world.

The Confidence of the Bible

All through its pages the Bible is confident that the reign of
God on the earth will come. "The earth," says Isaiah, "shall be
full of the knowledge of the Lord as the waters cover the sea"
(Is. 11:9).

"God is working His purpose out, as year succeeds to
    year:
God is working His purpose out, and the time is drawing
    near—
Nearer and nearer draws the time—the time that shall
    surely be
When the earth shall be filled with the glory of God, as
    the waters cover the sea."

Paul looked forward to the day when at the name of Jesus
every knee should bow, of things in heaven and things in
earth and things under the earth; and when every tongue will
confess that Jesus Christ is Lord to the glory of God the
Father (Phil. 2:10, 11). And above all, Jesus Himself had
that same confidence when he said, "I, when I am lifted up
from the earth, will draw all men to myself" (John 12:32).
All through the Bible there is this sense of the ultimate triumph

of God and the ultimate return of Jesus as King and Lord of all.

The Return of Jesus

One thing we must begin by laying down. When this consummation will come, when Jesus will return in power we do not know and we cannot know. When Jesus' disciples asked him after his resurrection if he was going to restore the Kingdom, his answer was, "It is not for you to know times or seasons which the Father has fixed by his own authority" (Act 1:7). Of the last days Jesus said, "But of that day and hour no one knows, not even the angels of heaven, nor the Son, but the Father only" (Matt. 24:36 cp. Mark 13:32). Even Jesus himself did not know when that final day of triumph would come.

Ourselves and the Return of Jesus

If that be so two things are to be said in regard to ourselves. (a) It is not only useless to speculate about it, it is actually blasphemous, for surely no one can think that what was hidden from Jesus will be revealed to him, and no man can think himself wiser than Jesus was. There has been a colossal amount of time and ingenuity and labour wasted in speculations regarding the Second Coming of our Lord. After Jesus himself has told us that he did not know that day or that hour we must rest content not to know and to leave matters to God. (b) But that very ignorance and that very uncertainty is the greatest reason for holding ourselves ready. The real man is the man who is prepared for every emergency; and the Christian is the man who is prepared for the greatest crisis of all. The best preparation of all is simply to go on faithfully and quietly doing our appointed work. Once in America there came a day of dreadful darkness so that men thought that the end of the world was coming. The senate was meeting at the time and many wished to abandon all business and to wait. But one who was wiser said, "Light the candles and let the business proceed, for how could our Lord better come upon us than doing our appointed work?" We must rest content not to know when the consummation comes; but we must accept that very uncertainty as a challenge that we may be found ready. Jesus said that the best servant is the servant who has all things ready whenever his Lord comes (Matt. 24:42, 51).

The Signs of the Kingdom

None the less there are signs that the Kingdom is on the way and that the King comes. Let us once again remember our definition—the Kingdom of God is a society upon earth where God's will is as perfectly done as it is in heaven. That is to say, the nearer the world is to doing God's will the nearer is the coming of the King. Sometimes people argue as to whether the world is getting better or worse. There is only one answer to that question. When Oliver Cromwell was arranging his son Richard's education, he said, "I would have him know a little history." And to anyone who knows history the world is getting better. Let us take some examples. More people know, and can know, about Jesus now than ever before. In the first six centuries of the history of the Church the New Testament was translated into six different languages; by the end of the first sixteen centuries it had only reached thirty different languages; but in our own day the New Testament exists in whole or in part in no fewer than one thousand one hundred and twenty different languages. The message of Jesus is spreading farther and farther abroad. The way in which people treat each other has improved beyond all knowledge. Seneca was the highest of all the Roman thinkers. He said things so wise and so noble that they would not be out of place in any Christian book. He lived at exactly the same time as Paul. Seneca writes in one of his letters: "We strangle a mad dog; we slaughter a fierce ox; we plunge the knife into a sickly cattle lest they taint the herd; *children who are born weakly and deformed we drown.*" In his day that was the natural thing to do; nobody looked on it even as out of place let alone cruel. We cannot conceive of that happening nowadays. Why? Not because the world is a fully Christian place yet, but because the influence of Jesus has so permeated society that that cannot happen. We have a letter written from a husband who is away on business to his wife. The letter was written in A.D. 1. It was dug up in the sands of Egypt and it can still be read just as it was written. It goes like this:

> "Hilarion to Alis, his wife, heartiest greetings, and to my dear Berous and Apollonarion. Know that we are still even now in Alexandria. Do not worry if when all the others return I remain in Alexandria. I beg and beseech you to take care of the little child, and as soon as we receive wages I will send them to you. If—good luck to you—you bear a child, if it is a boy, let it live, *if it is a girl, throw it out.* You told Aphrodisias, Do not forget me. How can I forget you? I beg you therefore not to worry."

It is a queer mixture of tender affection and utter callousness. In Roman times it was the regular routine thing to expose— that is, to throw away—unwanted children, especially girls. Even a Roman senator could say in the senate, "There is scarcely one of us here who has not ordered one or more of his infant children to be exposed to death." In Rome, when a child was born, the child was laid at the father's feet. If the father picked up the child that meant that he acknowledged the child and the child would be kept; if he refused to pick up the child, the child was exposed and thrown away to die. Once again, we cannot conceive of that happening today. Why? Again, not because the world is wholly Christian, but because the influence of Christianity has so permeated society that these things cannot happen. In Roman times a slave was classed as a living tool. He was a thing and had no rights whatever. Once a slave was carrying a precious goblet of wine to his master; he slipped and the goblet fell and broke. Immediately the master ordered him to be flung living into the fishpond in the centre of the courtyard where the savage lampreys tore him to pieces. It is impossible to imagine a master treating a servant like that nowadays. Even morally the world is getting better. Demosthenes, one of the great Greeks, wrote this: "We keep prostitutes for pleasure; we keep mistresses for the day-to-day needs of the body; we keep wives for the begetting of children and for the faithful guardianship of our homes." Lax as moral standards are today, we cannot conceive of any man in a public position, as Demosthenes was, laying down a principle like that as the ordinary accepted standard of morality. How can you say that the world is getting better, when so many thousands of people are still refugees with little hope of a real purpose in life or a country in which to live? The answer is simply this—that two thousand years ago the refugee problem would have produced no special reaction, and certainly no feeling of shock. The very fact that the conscience of the nations has been stirred is the proof that they have begun to judge things by the standards and in the light of Christ. The dawn does not break like a lightning flash or a clap of thunder; the flower does not emerge full grown the minute the seed is planted; the harvest does not ripen in a day. It all takes time for God's ways are not usually the sensational ways. The signs of the Kingdom are there; and for each one of them we should thank God, for each one of them brings the final consummation nearer.

Ourselves and the Triumph of the King

When we bring this down to ourselves two things emerge. (a) In a very real sense the Kingdom is God's. Without God we can do nothing. On his power and his help we depend entirely; but none the less we can hinder the coming of the Kingdom in all its full and final consummation. When God wants something done he works through men. The Church is the body of Christ. That is to say, we are literally hands to do Christ's work, feet to run upon His errands, lips to speak for him. When God wants a sick person cured he has to get a physician or a surgeon to heal him. When God wants a child taught he has to get a teacher to teach him. When God wants his message spread abroad he has to get men to tell it. Once Toscanini, the famous conductor, was rehearsing an orchestra. The orchestra was obviously not really trying. Toscanini laid down his baton and said quietly, "Gentlemen, God has told me how he wants this piece of music played and you—you hinder God." We can hinder God. God wants all men to know him and to love him. How can that be unless missionaries go out to the ends of the earth and unless we support them with our money and our prayers? God wants sick people healed, sad people comforted, poor people helped. How can that be unless we go about doing good? If God wants his praise sung, his children taught, he needs choir members, Sunday School teachers. That is our job. As someone said, God is everywhere looking for hands to use. The little jobs count just as much as the big jobs. He needs our hands and if we withhold them we hinder his work. (b) And that means, above all, that we can hasten the coming of the Kingdom and the great final triumph of Jesus by taking him ourselves as our Saviour, our Master and our Lord. Everyone who submits to Jesus entirely and completely is another citizen of the Kingdom. Everyone who does that helps God to bring the completion of his purpose a little nearer. It is a wonderful thing to feel that God wants us to be Christians *not only for our sakes but for his*; for God is Father, and God can never be content so long as one member of his family will not come home. We may not think that we can do much to help the final triumph of the King. One thing we can do—we can make him *our* King.

> "Brothers, this Lord Jesus
>   Shall return again,
> With His Father's glory,
>   With His angel train;
> For all wreaths of empire
>   Meet upon His brow
> And our hearts confess Him
>   King of glory now."

The Final Triumph of the King

The Christian view of history is that the world is on its way to a final goal when the kingdoms of the world shall be the Kingdom of the Lord, and when Jesus shall return. When that day will be it is useless to speculate for even Jesus did not know its date. But though we cannot tell when it will come we can strive to be ready for its coming. The Kingdom is on the way for there are signs that God's will slowly but inevitably is conquering amongst men. The Kingdom is God's; without him nothing can happen; but we can hinder the coming of the kingdom by failing to give ourselves to him to use. And in the last analysis our first duty is to make him King of *our* hearts and Lord of *our* lives.

QUESTIONS FOR DISCUSSION

1. What would you say to people who work out complicated calculations to fix the date of the Second Coming?

2. How can we best prepare for the Second Coming of Christ?

3. What does it mean to take Jesus as our Saviour, Master and Lord?